CLINICAL ORTHOPEDICS IN AYURVEDA

GIKKU ALIAS BENNY

BLUEROSE PUBLISHERS
India | U.K.

Copyright © Dr Gikku Alias Benny MS (Ay) 2024

All rights reserved by author. No part of this publication may be reproduced, stored in a retrieval system or transmitted in any form or by any means, electronic, mechanical, photocopying, recording or otherwise, without the prior permission of the author. Although every precaution has been taken to verify the accuracy of the information contained herein, the publisher assumes no responsibility for any errors or omissions. No liability is assumed for damages that may result from the use of information contained within.

BlueRose Publishers takes no responsibility for any damages, losses, or liabilities that may arise from the use or misuse of the information, products, or services provided in this publication.

For permissions requests or inquiries regarding this publication,
please contact:

BLUEROSE PUBLISHERS
www.BlueRoseONE.com
info@bluerosepublishers.com
+91 8882 898 898
+4407342408967

ISBN: 978-93-5989-755-4

Cover design: Muskan Sachdeva
Typesetting: Pooja Sharma

First Edition: January 2024

Dedication

This book is offered with thanks for

the deep affection of my family

the insight of my gurus

the gratefulness of my patients

the inspiration of my friends

the enthusiasm of my students

आचार्यात् पादमादत्ते पादं शिष्य स्वमेधया |
पादं सब्रह्मचारिभ्य: पादं काल क्रमेण च ||

FOREWORD

Dr Sudhikumar K B

Visiting Professor, KUHS

School of Fundamental Research in Ayurveda

Tripunithura

I congratulate Dr Gikku Alias Benny for publishing 'Clinical Orthopedics in Ayurveda – Cases and Insights', a book which shows his deep knowledge in Ayurveda orthopedics and his experience in this field. The aim of the book is to inspire the students and upcoming doctors to practice orthopedics. He described the ancient 'Bhagna chikitsa' of Susrutha in his book, which is relevant even today and compared it with modern orthopedic terminology for proper understanding.

He well described the applied anatomy of the shoulder, elbow, wrist, hand, knee, and ankle joint, explained all the common soft tissue injuries and pathologies of these joints. He shared the successful management of these as case presentations and QR code, so the doctors can easily follow them. His case presentation is unique as he successfully applied ayurveda management without compromising the fundamentals of ayurveda. He incorporated the 'marma chikitsa' of ayurveda for managing the sports injuries. Immediate pain and swelling reduction are a primary need of sports injury management, which he acquired with pricking and suction and by the proper use of 'Rakthamoksha and Agnikarma'. The use of X ray as an investigation technique is well explained for each joint, dislocation, and fracture, and indicated special investigation such as CT & MRI wherever essential. He explained the successful internal and external medication for these conditions.

As an experienced Professor in Salyatantra I hope he made this book with the willingness to share his knowledge to others who need it. Hence, I recommend this book as a must-read book for the students and young doctors who wants to pursue this field.

Dr Sudhikumar K B

Visiting Professor

PREFACE

विद्या ददाति विनयं विनयाद्याति पात्रताम् ।
पात्रत्वाद्धनमाप्नोति धनाद्धर्मं ततः सुखम् ॥

'Clinical Orthopedics in Ayurveda : Cases and Insights' is a book with concise knowledge on common orthopedic injuries and diseases. This textbook incorporates comprehensive information on clinical presentation, examination, evaluation and intervention of all musculoskeletal injuries and pathological conditions that an Ayurvedic clinician will encounter in their daily practice.

As I started my voyage to the world of 'Bhagna Chikitsa' as a Salyatantra postgraduate and later as a consultant, I had to spend endless hours exploring through a myriad of literature for the information I needed. The results of these long quests provided me with diverse concepts, while some textbooks delivered a detailed explanation on examination, others enlightened me on intervention. But the availability of 'all in one' books for Ayurvedic orthopedics practices and protocols were very limited. Over the years, I started compiling my own notes from all available resources and keeping records of the clinical cases I have come across.

The aim of this book is to fill a void in the present Ayurvedic orthopedic literature and to be of value to the budding doctors and clinicians. 60-80 percent cases approaching an ayurvedic practitioner comprises Orthopedic neurology and soft tissue injuries. Every clinician should focus on it, with proper diagnosis and assessment of prognosis and management with rehabilitation to achieve a favorable outcome. To identify the abnormal, it is often helpful to learn about the normal first. In this book each disease or injury description is aligned under the respective anatomical structure with a short introduction on the normal anatomy. An accurate diagnosis is the stepping stone towards a successful healing, which requires a systematic approach. This book attempts to bring to you the detailed assessment with lots of case scenarios, possible differential diagnosis, and appropriate diagrams. A correct diagnosis must be followed by a carefully planned management for a promising result. Thus, great emphasis is given in this book on the appropriate use of conservative management techniques and rehabilitation. The book on Ayurvedic clinical orthopedics is structured as follows:

Introduction:

- Brief overview of Ayurvedic clinical orthopedics.
- Introduction to basic terminologies in the field.

Diagnosis:
- In-depth exploration of clinical assessment techniques for orthopedic conditions.
- Discussion on the role of radiological studies in diagnosis.

Management Protocol:
- Conservative management approaches for fractures.
- Comprehensive notes on managing pathological diseases in orthopedics.

Joint-Specific Sections:
- Applied anatomy, clinical examination, common pathologies, injuries, radiology, and management of the following joints:
  - Shoulder
  - Elbow
  - Wrist
  - Temporomandibular (TMJ)
  - Knee
  - Ankle

Limitations and Referral:
- Discussion on challenges faced in conservative management.
- Identification of situations requiring referral to other specialties.

This structure provides a clear and organized flow, guiding readers from general concepts to specific joint details, making it a valuable resource for Ayurvedic practitioners and those interested in the integration of Ayurveda with orthopedic care.

QR code is given at the end of each section, which on opening will have the video of the respective module, with highlight on clinical examination.

I am indebted to many persons, who directly or indirectly take part in the completion of this book. This book is the handiwork after innumerable revisions and modifications since the last two years. My expectation is to bring out the revised new edition within 1 year. I am planning to bring another book on spinal injuries and pathology.

"The science of medicine is as incomprehensible as the ocean. It cannot be fully described even in hundreds and thousands of verses." - Sushrutha

Suggestions to improve the contents are always welcome.

Acknowledgments

I want to thank everyone who played a key role in making this Clinical Ayurveda in Orthopedics book a reality. Your contributions are deeply appreciated. I extend my sincere thanks to the patients who generously shared their real-life cases. Your contribution has provided valuable insights into the complexities of Ayurvedic interventions. Your resilience and trust have been the guiding force behind this project.

I express my heartfelt gratitude to all my teachers at Government Ayurveda College, Tripunithura, during both my graduation and post-graduation. Your collective wisdom has been instrumental in shaping my comprehensive understanding of Ayurveda in the context of orthopedic care.

Special thanks to Dr. Ramankutty Varier, Dr. C Sureshkumar, Dr. Jose T Paikada, Dr. G. Shyamkrishnan, Dr. M Prasad, Dr. Ajayan Sadanandan and Dr. Jomon Joseph Daniel for their inspiration and guidance throughout my practice. I extend my gratitude to my postgraduate colleagues, practitioners, and students who attended my classes.

I want to express my deepest gratitude to my friends and family, the greatest source of my energy. I am grateful for the blessings of my parents, Mr. Bennymon Varghese and Mrs. Lovely Cherian, and for the love and care of my wife, Mrs. Elsa Maria Mathews, and my children, Ephrem, Ezekiel, and Esther.

Furthermore, I would like to express my appreciation to the publisher, Bluerose, for their unwavering support and encouragement, which played a crucial role in bringing this project to fruition.

CONTRIBUTORS' LIST

Dr G CHANDRAKUMAR BAM, MD (Ay)
Retd Professor and Superintendent
Department of Shalya Tantra
Govt. Ayurveda College
Thiruvananthapuram

Dr MATHEWS JOSEPH VEMPILLY BAMS, MD (Ay)
Retd Specialist Marma Medical Officer
ISM department
Government of Kerala

Dr RAVISANKAR PERVAJE BAMS, MS (Ay)
Director and Chief Surgeon
Susrutha Ayurveda Hospital
Puthur, Mangalore

REVIEWERS

Dr SUDHIKUMAR K B BAM, MD (Ay)
Visiting Professor
Kerala University of Health Sciences (KUHS)
School of Fundamental Research in Ayurveda (SFRA)

Dr ARJUN VIJAY BAMS
PG Scholar
Department of Shalya Tantra
Govt. Ayurveda College
Thiruvananthapuram

CONTENT DEVELOPMENT

Dr CUKKU SARA BENNY MBBS , MD
Assistant professor
Department of Biochemistry

Ramaiah medical college
Bangalore

Dr KARTHIK K P BAMS, MD(Ay)
Phd Scholar
All India Institute of Ayurveda
New Delhi

Dr ATHUL MOHAN BAMS
CRAV scholar
Charaka Ayurveda Asramam
Secunderabad, Telangana

Dr MELVINA RAJU BAMS
Junior consultant
Vettukattil Ayurveda Hospital
Muvattupuzha

Dr ANITTA P ELDHOSE BAMS
Junior consultant
Vettukattil Ayurveda Hospital
Muvattupuzha

Review of Clinical Orthopedics in Ayurveda : Cases and Insights

'Clinical Orthopedics in Ayurveda : Cases and Insights' is an attempt of a clinician to translate the available textual knowledge into practice. The author focuses on fracture, dislocation, and joint pathology of upper and lower limbs. The objective of the book is to familiarise the "Bhagna chikitsa" of Ayurveda after gaining the contemporary orthopaedic knowledge and disseminate it to ayurvedic practitioners. Making them able to handle soft tissue injuries, sports injuries, and neurological problem arising from these injuries.

In the introduction chapter "Brief overview of Ayurvedic clinical orthopedics" the author compiled almost all references from ayurvedic orthopaedics of acharyas of ayurveda especially Susrutha. The ancient wisdom of ayurveda bhagna chikitsa is relevant even today, during Samhita period, Susrutha classified bhagna into dislocation and fracture only through observing the presenting clinical symptoms without any radiological investigation. By comparing the classification of fracture described by Susrutha to the modern classification, students will be able to find how accurately the ancient texts have described it. The book has incorporated "marma chikitsa" (the unique treatment in ayurveda), injury management, particularly dealing with sports injury. The use of rakthamoksha and agnikarma to reduce acute pain management has also been well described.

In 'Introduction to basic terminologies in the field' explains the basics of body planes and the basic terminology for the assistance of readers. Basics of fracture diagnosis and management, classification of fracture as per Susrutha and Madhavakara has also been described in this chapter. In the chapter basic of clinical examination, describes the features of fracture and dislocation and special clinical examination wherever it is needed. Radiological investigation in fracture with well explaining its different views for the proper understanding of practitioners is also mentioned. The use of special investigation, (where to use CT and where to use MRI) is limited to where exactly needed. General management and specific management are well described. The management of soft tissue injuries and neurological involvement correction are explained. The method of immobilization, rules of bandages, its clinical application, the importance and need of rehabilitation, clinical application of orthosis, internal medication, and pathya and apathya are well described. While describing the management protocol for pathological conditions the author explains it into five sections starting from amapachana to rehabilitation. The chapter gives a clear direction how to correct sports injuries. Here the author quotes the management protocol of raktavruta vata prakopa.

The next section 'Individual joint' started with shoulder joint, for better understanding a description of the applied anatomy of the joint and muscles supporting the function of shoulder joint was provided. It then described the clinical examination of muscles, particularly the rotator cuff, which will be the most effected for the origin of shoulder joint pain. While describing clinical examination the author explained all the physical tests to confirm the diagnosis. Explained the stability of the joint and range of movement. Common pathology of shoulder joint was explained with the help of a case presentation. It then described the shoulder joint injuries, examination, and management (more on QR code). Dislocation of the joint and correction methods were also clearly explained. For the investigation of these, the author described X ray and its different views to visualise properly and the clinical tests to check the stability of the joint. All three types of dislocation and recurrent dislocation were explained and the ayurvedic management for these are well stated. The correction methods of these were given as QR code for better understanding for the young practitioner. Further, the author described the possible sports injuries to this joint and how to manage this. Finally, the author summarised the pathologies and injuries with the help of case presentations.

The chapter 'Elbow joint' began with applied anatomy, then the physical examination and the importance of joint palpation. The clinical examination of the joint including the vascular and neurological assessment as both the vessels and nerves can be involved in the injury of this joint has been described. The types of dislocation possible and its reduction methods are explained with the help of QR code. The possible pathology and its management has been well explained.

'Wrist and hand' applied anatomy, followed by examination of injuries, investigations, particularly X ray and its possible views to visualise carpal bones are well described. The author described the management of fracture and dislocation such as scaphoid fracture, boxers' fracture, lunate dislocation, mallet finger. The colles' fracture diagnosis and management has been explained as a case presentation. Bandages and use of orthosis for the wrist joint has been described. The pathologies of this joint are well said and the most common pathology 'Carpal tunnel syndrome' explained in detail and its successful management technique of pricking and suction. De-Quervain's, Carpal Tunnel Syndrome, ayurveda management are explained.

The author further described the Temporomandibular joint dislocation and its successful reduction method is explained and the reference from ayurveda are quoted.

'Knee joint' explanation started with applied anatomy and more importance were given to the ligaments of the knee joint, the collateral and capsular ligament, and the meniscus as these are more vulnerable to injury. Physical examination of the joint by palpation of the anatomical important areas, the bursa around the knee joint has been described. Then the stability of the joint and range of motion checking with different tests were mentioned. The

ACL, PCL and meniscal injuries are well said as these can be mostly affected in sports injury. Its examination and investigation are well said. The management of these injuries, its immobilisation by bandages and use of proper orthosis are clearly described. The commonest pathology of knee joint is the OA knee. It is well described and investigation of x-ray and how to grade OA by radiology, the differential diagnosis of OA with RA both by the symptoms and radiological are explained. The another pathology Osgood Schlatter Disease (OSG), how to differentiate from Sinding-Larsen-Johansson syndrome and differentiate from patellar tendonitis are explained with case presentation and its successful ayurveda management is explained. Osteochondritis Dissecans (OCD) has also been explained as a case presentation. Ilio tibial band syndrome (ITBS) was explained with clinical examination tests and its management. To relieve immediate pain and tenderness the use of rakthamoksha and successful use of agnikarma were described. Chondromalacia patella was described along with an explanation on how to make use of clinical tests for better diagnosis, management has been explained as a case presentation. The rehabilitation of knee joint in different conditions are well explained and as usual the author summarised the important examinations to remember as concluding remarks of the chapter.

'Ankle joint' started with applied anatomy, physical and clinical examination of stability and range of motion. Radiological investigation with X ray of ankle joint, calcaneus, metatarsal and alignment of foot were described. It then explained the differential diagnosis LCL Sprain, distal end tibial fracture, distal end fibula fracture and march fracture. It has explained the examination of pathology and ayurveda management, bandage techniques and rehabilitation, specifically the period of immobilisation for metatarsal fracture, tibial, fibular fracture, calcaneal fracture and LCL sprain were mentioned, the Grade I & II can be managed with ayurveda and Grade III with surgery.

Tarsal tunnel syndrome diagnosis and management were explained and OTTAWA rule of ankle were well said. A case presentation of metatarsal fracture was also added in this chapter. Rehabilitation of ankle joint has been explained. The chapter was concluded with the limitations of ayurveda doctors and mentioning the must referral situations for surgical correction.

The section, 'Formulations and procedures useful for musculoskeletal pathologies', listed 12 kashaya, some of them indicated in acute and chronic conditions, five most effective Eranda yoga, most effective four Gulika, eleven Sneha which can be used orally or as matrabasti, twelve either formulation or can be used as single drug which are having rasayana property (which is a plus point of this book), for the use of external application in acute injury Murivenna can be used and Nagaradi lepa in contusion, which are most effective. The author recommends some procedures like upanaha to reduce swelling, seka with dhanyamla, Kashaya, ksheera and taila according to the condition to relieve the pain. The author added the formulation of Murivenna, Nagaradi lepa, Grahadhoomadi lepa, Ellum nisadi choorna lepa which are Malayalam yoga for the proper understanding of Ayurveda practitioners.

The author explained all the major joint common injuries and pathologies of upper and lower limb except the hip joint. In pathological condition it would have been better if the author suggested other haematological investigations or urine examinations. The author sticks on the X ray investigation of the joints; it would have been better if the author suggested MRI for ligament injuries and meniscal injuries and explained with illustrations (CT will be more useful in ankle joint alignment of tarsal and meta tarsal bones). While describing the management it is better to mention the dose and frequency of internal medication and duration of use. Even though some of them are explained in QR code presentations, it would have been better to keep them in the book itself. It would have better to avoid Sanskrit sloka in between the English paragraphs, it can slow the pace of reading the book (a good practice would be to provide them as footnote). The placement of Temporomandibular dislocation shows some inconsistency with the rest of the text.

I congratulate Dr Gikku Alias Benny for his attempt to publish a book like Clinical orthopaedic in Ayurveda, clubbing his academic knowledge and his practical experience. His case presentations are unique and will be helpful for the students and upcoming ayurveda doctors. Hence, I strongly recommend this book to all those who are in orthopedic practice.

Dr Sudhikumar K B

Visiting Professor

KUHS- School of Fundamental Research in Ayurveda

Tripunithura.

Contents

1. INTRODUCTION 1
2. BASIC TERMINOLOGY IN ORTHOPEDICS 4
3. BASICS OF FRACTURE DIAGNOSIS AND MANAGEMENT 6
4. SHOULDER JOINT 34
5. ELBOW JOINT 85
6. WRIST JOINT AND HAND 100
7. TEMPOROMANDIBULAR JOINT (TMJ) DISLOCATION REDUCTION METHOD 113
8. KNEE JOINT 114
9. ANKLE JOINT 161
CONCLUSION 177
SUMMARY 178
REFERENCE 179
BIBLIOGRAPHY 180
FORMULATIONS AND PROCEDURES USEFUL FOR MUSCULOSKELETAL PATHOLOGIES 181

1. INTRODUCTION

Acharya Susruta, often referred to as the Father of Surgery, has provided practical insights into orthopedics and anorectal diseases. His management protocols for these conditions are not only scientifically sound but also highly effective and beneficial across various aspects such as time, functional outcomes, cost, and recurrence.

Even in today's era, the etiology, clinical features, and general management protocols outlined by Acharya Susruta remain relevant. His expertise is evident in examples like hastha tala bhagna, hanu sandhi vislesha, and koorpara sandhi vislesha, which are part of the rehabilitation process.

What's remarkable is that Acharya Susruta could diagnose fracture patterns without the need for modern radiological investigations, showcasing his clinical acumen. However, it's essential for us to apply these principles in practice rather than just boasting about them for the betterment of society.

This book acts as a bridge between ancient and modern practices, offering a unique perspective on special procedures that continue to influence the treatment of fractures. It serves as a valuable resource for both practitioners and enthusiasts. Emphasizing both theoretical and practical knowledge, Acharya Susruta and Vagbhata highlight the importance of a thorough clinical examination and hands-on experience for precision in healthcare practices.

इति शास्त्रेण यदृष्टं दृष्टं प्रत्यक्षतश्च यत्|

समागतं तदुभयं भूयो ज्ञानं विवर्धयेत् (A.S SU 34)

This book brings together ancient Ayurvedic wisdom and modern orthopedics, providing a complete guide to managing injuries. It dispels myths, explores rehabilitation strategies, and uses real-life cases to illustrate Ayurvedic approaches. Discover how to blend traditional wisdom with evidence-based methods to effectively treat injuries. The book showcases practical applications through case studies, demonstrating how Ayurvedic principles can be used in personalized care plans for musculoskeletal issues. It's a captivating journey into the synergy of ancient and contemporary healing practices.

This book explores basic principles and advanced practices, showing how theory and hands-on experience come together. It emphasizes the crucial role of clinical examination for healthcare professionals, illustrating its importance in accurate diagnosis and informed treatment planning. The book is a guide for aspiring practitioners, emphasizing the transformative impact when theory, practice, and clinical skills harmonize. While relevant investigations are necessary, the book encourages enthusiasm for diagnosing before relying solely on tests. It's a practical and engaging approach to mastering healthcare.

When it comes to medical tests, having some basic knowledge is important. For assessing knee osteoarthritis, it's recommended to order a standing Antero-Posterior (AP) view. It's essential to be graded using the Kellgren and Lawrence system for classification of osteoarthritis (KL scale). For fractures like in the calcaneus or scaphoid, knowing which special views to prescribe is crucial. It's a simple way to ensure the right tests are done for accurate diagnosis.

Understanding the prognosis of each medical situation based on our management is crucial. Unlike conventional medicine, outcomes can vary, so it's important to constantly improve and update our knowledge for better patient care. Staying informed allows us to adapt and enhance our approach to different situations.

सतताध्ययनं वादः परतन्त्रावलोकनम् |

तद्विद्याचार्यसेवा च बुद्धिमेधाकरो गणः (Su chi 28)

Our approach to healthcare must always be ethical. According to the esteemed Vaidyabhushana K Raghavan Thirumulpad sir, to maintain ethical practice, being scientific in our practice is essential. This means using technical terms (sva samnja) to communicate results effectively with fellow doctors. The book outlines a time-tested protocol tailored for treating injuries and pathologies, emphasizing the application of marmahata chikitsa in sports injuries. Dive into the world of sports injury management, where Ayurvedic wisdom meets modern sports medicine practices. Real cases help grasp the practical challenges involved.

Acharya Susruta's special procedures, known as Anusastra, are really helpful for fast pain relief and reversing health issues. By using these techniques, it's possible to cut down on time, costs, and the amount of medicine needed to a minimum.

Understanding rehabilitation as a crucial part of overall care, this narrative explores how blending rehabilitation principles enriches the holistic approach to patient well-being. It highlights the importance of a comprehensive rehabilitation framework, offering a transformative journey for both practitioners and patients. This work acts as a guide, navigating through medical education, clinical application, and the rehabilitative pathway, showcasing the profound impact rehabilitation can have on restoring health, functionality, and quality of life.

Utilizing rehabilitation effectively is key for assessing functional outcomes post-injury and maintaining relief in pathological diseases. After surgeries, incorporating rehabilitation principles promptly preserves range of motion. Teaming up with an orthopedic surgeon, skilled physiotherapist, dietitian, yoga and psychology consultant can significantly benefit patients. Teamwork proves highly effective in both injuries and chronic autoimmune conditions.

Pain serves as a crucial psychophysical response, acting as an imperative protective reflex. It signals distress or harm. It's essential to recognize and address the psychological dimension of pain in deserving patients. Refrain from disregarding individuals without discernible organic lesions during clinical examinations, acknowledging that pain experiences can manifest without explicit structural pathology. Embracing a comprehensive approach to pain management entails considering both the physical and psychological aspects for a more nuanced understanding and effective intervention.

Patients are our best teachers if we're open to learning. Clinical practice is an ongoing learning journey that never stops. Adidhi, Bodha, Acharana, and Pracharana are systematic methods we should follow for our own improvement as clinicians. This approach is not just for ourselves but also empowers our colleagues.

This guide isn't just a theoretical discussion; it's a practical roadmap for both practitioners and enthusiasts. "Ayurvedic Orthopaedics" is a valuable resource that blends Ayurvedic philosophy with real-world cases, providing an integrative and effective approach to musculoskeletal health and sports injury management. In the ever-evolving field of healthcare, the book explores the connection between scientific rigor and ethical practices. It stands as a testament to the transformative potential when scientific excellence and unwavering ethical commitments work hand in hand, guiding practitioners dedicated to healing with integrity.

.

2. BASIC TERMINOLOGY IN ORTHOPEDICS

3 planes

* Coronal - divides body into 2 equal halves, i.e. anterior and posterior.

*Sagittal - divides body into right and left halves through the middle of the body

*Axial (Transverse / horizontal view)- divides body into superior and inferior halves.

- Proximal :- is near to the heart
- Distal :- away from the heart
- Active Range Of Motion - the patient's muscles move the joint.
- Passive Range Of Motion - outside force moves the joint.
- sclerotic - increased bone density

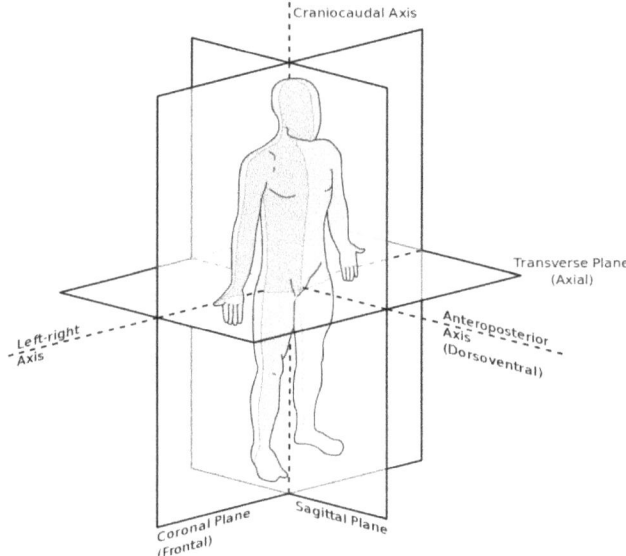

- lytic — bone destruction
- cortex — compact (dense) bone forming the bone surface
- medulla — trabecular bone in the bone marrow
- articular — refers to a joint (an articulation)
- demineralization — decreased bone density (as occurs with osteomalacia/osteopenia/osteoporosis)
- ankylosis — fusion
- osteo — prefix meaning bony (e.g. osteosarcoma)

- chondro — prefix meaning cartilaginous (e.g. chondrosarcoma)
- fibro — prefix meaning fibrous (e.g. fibrosarcoma)
- arthro — prefix meaning joint (e.g. arthritis)
- spondylo — prefix meaning spinal (e.g. spondyloarthropathy)
- dactyl — prefix meaning digit (either finger or toe, e.g. dactylitis)

3. BASICS OF FRACTURE DIAGNOSIS AND MANAGEMENT

- Fracture is a break in the continuity of bone, it may be complete or incomplete.
- Strain – a break in the continuity of muscle
- Sprain - a break in the continuity of ligament

Etiologically fracture is classified into

1. **Traumatic**
2. **Fatigue**
3. **Pathological**

Traumatic fractures occur due to trauma and can be again divided into

1. Direct
2. Indirect

- Direct fracture is fracture due to direct injury

Eg- nightstick fracture - fracture of ulna occurring while blocking a stick

- Indirect fracture is fracture due to transmitted force

Eg- clavicle fracture at the junction of medial two-third and lateral one-third due to fall on an outstretched hand (FOOSH)

Fatigue fractures

- (march fracture or stress fracture) is due to repetitive strain injury (RSI).

E.g.- neck of second and third metatarsal fracture due to RSI

Pathological fractures

- Fracture occurring due to trivial force or trauma. Bone is weakened due to a primary cause and management should be focused on primary disease.

Can be subdivided into 4

1. Congenital - osteogenesis imperfecta
2. Inflammatory – Tuberculosis, mostly thoracic vertebrae affected
3. Neoplastic – On metastasis from prostate cancer in males and breast cancer in females, Vertebrae, proximal one third of humerus and femur are commonly affected.
4. Insufficiency - osteoporosis, osteomalacia

Out of the 3 divisions in etiological classification, Acharya Susrutha only explains traumatic fracture.

पतनपीडनप्रहाराक्षेपणव्यालमृगदशनप्रभृतिभिरभिघातविशेषैरनेकविधमस्थनां भङ्गमुपदिशन्ति ||(SU. NI 15)

Fracture is again classified based on relation with external environment

1. Open or compound
2. Closed or simple

This division is seen in **Madhava nidanam** as **savruna** bhagna and **avruna** bhagna

There is another classification of fracture based on pattern

1. Transverse
2. Spiral
3. Oblique
4. Comminuted
5. Compression
6. Greenstick
7. Stellate

These patterns, are explained by Acharya Susrutha:

विशेषस्तु सम्मूढमुभयतोऽस्थि मध्ये भग्नं ग्रन्थिरिवोन्नतं कर्कटकम्, अश्वकर्णवदुद्नतमश्वकर्णकं, स्पृश्यमानं शब्दवच्चूर्णितमवगच्छेत्, पिच्चितं पृथुतां गतमनल्पशोफं, पार्श्वयोरस्थि हीनोद्नतमस्थिच्छलितं, वेल्लते प्रकम्पमानं काण्डभग्नम्, अस्थ्यवयवोऽस्थिमध्यमनुप्रविश्य मज्जानमुन्नह्लतीति मज्जानुगतम्, अस्थि निःशेषतश्छिन्नमतिपातितम्, आभुग्नमविमुक्तास्थि वक्रम्, अन्यतरपार्श्वविशिष्टं छिन्नं, पाटितमणुबहुविदारितं वेदनावच्च, शूकपूर्णमिवाध्मातं विपुलं विस्फुटितं स्फुटितमिति (SU.NI 15)

Bhagna	Most equivalent clinical condition	Site of fracture - example
Karkatakam	Stellate fracture	Skull, body of scapula
Aswakarnakam	Oblique fracture	Distal fibula
Choornitham	Comminuted fracture	Olecranon process
Pichitham	Compression fracture	T12 anterior wedge compression fracture
Asthichalitham	Avulsion fracture	Medial malleolus avulsion fracture due to deltoid ligament

Kandabhagnam	Transverse fracture	Shaft of tibia
Majjanugatham	Impacted fracture	Neck of femur
Athipathitham	Complete fracture	Displaced fracture
Vakram	Greenstick fracture	Radius fracture in children
Chinnam	Incomplete fracture	Torus or buckle
Patitham	Crack fracture	Hairline fracture
Sphutitham	Fissured fracture	Longitudinal fracture

Note:

In torus fractures (buckle fractures), there is a bulging of the cortex. In greenstick fractures, there is bowing with cortical disruption of only one side of the bone.

Clinical features of fracture includes

- Pain
- Tenderness
- Swelling
- Crepitus
- Bruising
- Deformity
- Loss of function

Acharya Susrutha explained the samanya lakshana as:

श्वयथुबाहुल्यं स्पन्दनविवर्तनस्पर्शासहिष्णुत्वमवपीड्यमाने शब्दः स्रस्ताङ्गता विविधवेदनाप्रादुर्भावः सर्वास्ववस्थासु न शर्मलाभ इति समासेन काण्डभग्नलक्षणमुक्तम् (SU.NI 15)

The cardinal features of a dislocation are,

- Deformity
- Loss of Function
- Severe Pain and Tenderness

Susrutha's recognition of these cardinal features reflects the timeless nature of these clinical signs, which continue to be fundamental aspects of diagnosing dislocations in contemporary medicine.

तत्र प्रसारणाकुञ्चनविवर्तनाक्षेपणशक्तिरुग्ररुजत्वं स्पर्शासहत्वं चेति सामान्यं सन्धिमुक्तलक्षणमुक्तम् (SU.NI 15)

BASIC CLINICAL EXAMINATION

- A **detailed history** is a crucial aspect of the diagnostic process in both injury and pathological conditions, including orthopedic issues. It's suggestive to follow this protocol:

1. Mechanism of Injury (Injury Conditions):
   - Understanding how the injury occurred is vital. Was it a fall, direct impact, overuse, or a sports-related incident? Knowing the mechanism helps in identifying potential structures affected and the nature of the injury.

2. Pathology and Etiological Factors (Pathological Conditions):
   - For non-traumatic orthopedic conditions, gathering information on the development of symptoms, the duration of the issue, and any underlying health conditions is crucial. Exploring factors such as family history, lifestyle, and occupation can provide valuable insights.

3. Pain Characteristics:
   - Describing the nature, location, and intensity of pain helps in pinpointing potential causes. Understanding factors that alleviate or exacerbate the pain is equally important.

4. Past Medical History:
   - Identifying any pre-existing medical conditions, surgeries, or relevant medical history contributes to a holistic understanding of the patient's health.

5. Medication and Allergies:
   - Knowing the patient's current medications and any history of allergies is important for planning treatment approaches and avoiding adverse reactions.

6. Lifestyle and Occupation:
   - Understanding the patient's daily activities, occupation, and lifestyle habits is essential for assessing factors that may contribute to or exacerbate orthopedic conditions.

7. Systemic Symptoms:
   - In some cases, systemic symptoms such as fever, weight loss, or changes in appetite may be indicative of underlying systemic conditions affecting the musculoskeletal system.

A thorough history provides a foundation for the subsequent physical examination, diagnostic tests, and the formulation of an appropriate treatment plan.

The basic orthopedic examination encompasses several crucial components:

Darsana (Look/Inspection):
- Visual assessment of the affected area for any visible deformities, swelling, discoloration, or abnormalities.

Sparsana (Feel/Palpation):
- Hands-on examination involving palpation to elicit tenderness, swelling, warmth, or abnormalities in the tissues, joints, or bones.

Prasna (History Taking and assessment of Range of Motion):
- Gathering information through patient history, focusing on the mechanism of injury, pathology, postural defects, etiological factors, and repetitive strain injuries (RSI).
- Assessing the range of motion by asking the patient to perform specific movements.

Special Clinical Examination:
- Conducting additional targeted examinations based on the suspected condition, which may involve specific tests and maneuvers to evaluate joint stability, muscle strength, and functional limitations.

Basic Radiological Investigations:
- Ordering and analyzing X-rays to obtain detailed images of the affected area for a more accurate diagnosis.

Newer Imaging Techniques (if needed):
- Utilizing advanced imaging techniques, such as CT scans and MRI scans when necessary for a comprehensive assessment.

Comparison with the Normal Limb:
- Always compare the affected limb or joint with the unaffected or normal side to identify any asymmetry, differences in range of motion, or abnormalities.

  This systematic approach ensures a thorough examination and helps in formulating an accurate diagnosis.

Inspection (Look):
- General alignment, deformity, shortening, swelling, and skin color assessment are crucial. The comparison with the unaffected side helps identify asymmetries or abnormalities.

Palpation (Feel):
- Palpating the skin temperature, bones, soft tissues, and identifying local tenderness provides information about the condition of the affected area.

Range of motion (move):
- Assessing the range of active and passive movements is fundamental. Differentiating between passive and active movements helps identify whether restrictions are due to pain or other factors.

Measurement:
- Comparing measurements on both sides helps identify discrepancies in length or size, which can be indicative of various musculoskeletal conditions.

CLINICAL DIAGNOSIS OF FRACTURE

1. **Bony Tenderness and Irregularity:**
   - Bony tenderness and irregularity are typical features of fractures. Palpating the affected area for tenderness and checking for any irregularities in the bone's surface can strongly indicate a fracture.

2. **Springing Test:**
   - The springing test is a useful diagnostic maneuver. Squeezing the proximal end and eliciting pain at the distal end suggests a potential fracture.

3. **Tenderness from Multiple Directions:**
   - Assessing tenderness from different directions after an injury is a clever diagnostic strategy. If tenderness persists regardless of the direction (ventrally, dorsally, or laterally), it suggests a fracture. In contrast, if tenderness is directional, it might indicate a contusion rather than a fracture.

INVESTIGATIONS

Includes basic radiological investigations, newer imaging techniques and basic haematological investigations.

X-RAY INVESTIGATION

Radiological investigation - basics

- Clinical Examination Precedes X-ray:
  - Clinical examination is a prerequisite before advising an X-ray. Understanding the patient's symptoms and conducting a physical examination helps guide the decision to pursue imaging.
- Consider Bilateral X-ray:
  - When needed, a bilateral X-ray should be advised. This approach helps establish a baseline for comparison and aids in identifying any asymmetries or abnormalities.
- Special Views Based on Condition:

- Special views should be advised based on the specific condition. Tailoring the imaging approach to the suspected pathology ensures a more accurate diagnosis.
- Avoid Unnecessary Views:
  - It's essential never to advise a view if it is not needed. Minimizing unnecessary radiation exposure is a crucial aspect of responsible and patient-centered care.
- Use of Oblique Views:
  - The oblique view is recommended in specific situations, such as for assessing the scaphoid, spondylolisthesis, and cervical spine. These views provide additional information that may not be visible in standard views.
- Post-Reduction Check X-ray:
  - After reduction procedures, a check X-ray should be taken. This helps confirm the success of the reduction and ensures proper alignment.

Rule of 2
- Two sides – for comparison (needed to rule out fracture in children below the age of 16-19 before completion of ossification and congenital conditions like congenital bipartite patella)
- Two views – AP & Lateral (or according to site)
- Two joints – proximal & distal joints if needed
- Two times – before & after treatment or reduction

Special views
- Patella – skyline view
- Shoulder – axillary and transscapular (Y) view
- Calcaneus – axial view
- Scaphoid – scaphoid view (Wrist PA with ulnar deviation)

NEWER IMAGING TECHNIQUES

According to need (for example fracture of pelvis, proximal tibia fracture), advice further imaging techniques

CT is advisable for
- Bone (fracture) and bleed (intracranial)
- 3D CT is helpful in displaced fractures

MRI is advised in
- Soft tissue injuries
- Stress fracture (march or fatigue fracture)

NOTE: **Never advise CT where MRI is needed.**

ULTRASOUND SONOGRAPHY

USG is recommended in musculoskeletal conditions of the shoulder to rule out rotator cuff tears and tendonitis. It's found effective to detect biceps tendonitis and subacromial bursitis. Ultrasound is useful in detecting acromioclavicular joint arthritis.

In the knee joint, it helps to rule out synovial cysts, medial collateral ligament and lateral collateral ligament tears. Ultrasound is also used in diagnosis of patellar and quadriceps tears. Ultrasound can suggest an early diagnosis of osteoarthritis by demonstrating joint effusion, synovial thickening, bony changes and articular cartilage changes.

NB. When compared to MRI, USG is cheaper, but to visualise an intra articular structure or larger areas of soft tissues, muscles, or cartilage, an MRI is a better diagnostic tool than USG.

HAEMATOLOGICAL INVESTIGATIONS

Basic haematological investigations are advisable to rule out systemic illness associated with soft tissue rheumatism. It includes:

Blood
- CBC
- ESR
- CRP
- URIC ACID
- SERUM CALCIUM
- LIVER FUNCTION TEST

ANA, ACCP are advised in patients based on raised inflammatory markers (CRP and ESR) on basic haematological investigations and when it demands clinically with multiple joint involvement and systemic illness.

NB. For the diagnosis of rheumatoid arthritis, it's advisable to follow the modified ACR/EULAR criteria.

MANAGEMENT PROTOCOL OF ACUTE INJURY (HOT ORTHOPEDICS)

Primary care

PRICE
- **P**rotection
- **R**est
- **I**ce
- **C**ompression
- **E**levation

POLICE
- **P**rotection
- **O**ptimal Loading
- **I**ce
- **C**ompression
- **E**levation

NO HARM
- **No H**eat
- **No A**lcohol
- **No R**e-injury
- **No M**assage

Definitive care management of injury

3 Rs
- **R**eduction (**REDUCE**)
- **R**etention / immobilization (**HOLD**)
- **R**ehabilitation (**MOVE**)

As per Acharya Susrutha

आच्छनैः पीडनैश्चैव सङ्क्षेपैर्बन्धनैस्तथा (SU.CHI 3)

Out of 3 Rs, the most important one is rehabilitation.

Reduction is needed only in displaced conditions or dislocations. The reduction should be specific and gentle. Before attempting the reduction method, we should diagnose the condition clinically and radiologically.

Reduction includes
- Traction
- Counter-traction
- Correction

As per Acharya Susrutha,

अवनामितमुन्नह्येदुन्नतं चावपीडयेत् ॥

आच्छेदतिक्षिप्तमधो गतं चोपरि वर्तयेत् (SU.CHI 3)

The second one is retention/ immobilization. Immobilization is not needed in all injuries. But rehabilitation is essential always.

Rehabilitation

Orthopedic Rehabilitation:

Orthopedic rehabilitation is a powerful tool for restoring normal life after injury. Whether patient's seek to return to everyday activities or competitive sports, this targeted approach surely help them to achieve their goals within a reasonable timeframe.

NOTE: After removing the bandage from the affected side, rehabilitation to that particular site shall be started. Actually, rehab begins from the very first day in all injuries. For example, in the case of a Colles' fracture, the rehabilitation process addresses the fingers, elbow, and shoulder from the first day of wrist immobilization. Whenever there is absence of tenderness over fracture site, the wrist bandage is typically removed within 4-6 weeks. Following principles of rehabilitation, it's feasible to restore ROM of wrist by following a step by step approach.

Principles of rehabilitation includes:

1. Upanaha:

After removing bandages, lepa or upanaha can help reduce swelling, if present. As it is a case of injury, nagaradi lepa offers a safe and effective option.

2. Dhara (Seka):

Once swelling subsides, dhara can be introduced. Dhanyamla dara is advisable in the initial phase followed by taila dhara. Asavenna, pinda taila, or taila with amla rasa and lavana rasa, chinchadi and parinata keri ksheeradi taila are better choices for reducing stiffness and promoting flexibility.

3. Vyayama (Active Use and Exercise):

This is the bedrock of orthopedic rehabilitation, encompassing various stages of movement progression:

Mobilization: Using mrit pinda dharana (soft mud) allows gentle movement and mobilization.

Active Use and Exercise against Resistance: This stage involves using lavana pinda dharana to provide controlled resistance, similar to resistance bands or therabands in physiotherapy.

Active Use and Exercise with Weight Bearing: Progressing to pashana pinda dharana introduces weight bearing, simulating real-life activities and strengthening muscles.

उभे तले समे कृत्वा तलभग्नस्य देहिनः |

बध्नीयादामतैलेन परिषेकं च कारयेत् ||

मृत्पिण्डं धारयेत् पूर्वं **लवणं** च ततः परम् |

हस्ते जातबले चापि कुर्यात् **पाषाणधारणम्** (SU.CHI 3)

MANAGEMENT OF IMMOBILIZATION OF INJURIES AND SIGNIFICANCE OF SEETHA-USHNA (COLD- HOT) APPROACH

The duration of immobilization varies based on factors such as age, gender, and the affected structure. A fracture refers to a break in bone continuity, a strain is a break in muscle continuity, a sprain is a break in ligament continuity, and an abrasion is a break in skin continuity.

When a bone is fractured, it tends to have more hematoma due to its high vascularity when compared to a ligament sprain. This is the reason for swayathur bahulya after bhagna. This hematoma serves dual purpose: acting as a temporary splint and aiding in the second phase of fracture healing.

The stages of fracture healing include

1. Stage of **hematoma formation**
2. Stage of **cellular proliferation or granulation tissue formation**
3. Stage of **callus formation**
4. Stage of **remodeling** (Continues for months to years after clinical union)

The overall process of fracture healing can be categorized into three stages:

1. **Inflammatory**
2. **Reparative**
3. **Remodelling**

The Seetha and Ushna management approach is crucial in addressing the symptoms in the initial phase associated with fractures and functional outcome in the later phase, respectively.

The cellular proliferation stage, the second phase of fracture healing, is initiated by hematoma formation. Open fractures lacking hematoma, may experience delayed healing. In closed fractures, hematoma acts as a foreign body, causing soft tissue injury and swelling. To address the resulting pitta rakta kopa, sheeta prayoga is recommended.

Sheeta prayoga, using Murivenna, helps reduce complications, initial pain, and swelling in injuries. Murivenna, containing 4 sheetha and 4 teekshna ingredients in a kera base, is suitable for pacifying symptoms in the initial phase of fractures and burns. Except for contusions, which benefit from Nagaradi lepa or Karutha Marma Vattu application over affected site, all other acute injury conditions require immobilization to reduce swelling and ensure healing.

For upper limb injuries, it's suggested to use a sling. For lower limb injuries, elevate the limb by 15 cm. This reduces swelling, and immediate lepa is not necessary before immobilization. During the initial phase, immobilize with Murivenna until callus formation. After this, transition from seetha prayoga to ushna prayoga as part of the rehabilitation process.

In specific fractures like undisplaced lower limb fractures, it's better to remove the bandage in 8 to 12 weeks based on clinical assessment of callus formation and absence of tenderness. For a radius bone fracture, consider removing the bandage within 4 to 6 weeks.

- In a grade 1 ligament tear, it's advisable to remove the bandage when tenderness is absent within 7 to 10 days and shift to rehabilitation.
- For a grade 2 ligament tear, the bandage comes off after 21 days, and then the hot application treatments start.
- The transition from cold to warm depends on the affected structure.
- For a grade 1 muscle strain, ushna prayoga may be advised after 72 hours.
- In a fracture, after callus formation, it's recommended to switch from sheeta to ushna prayoga.
- Tenderness serves as the indicator to assess callus formation.

If a patient shows up at the orthopedic clinic with a limp due to an anterior talofibular ligament injury that happened 6 or 7 months ago, it suggests they might have initially consulted a non-professional or a quack. Most probably the massage which was applied, disrupted the hematoma and caused delayed healing. The takeaway: avoid massaging in the early stages of an acute injury and do proper immobilization for proper healing.

Methods of immobilization

1. External splinting- pop, splinted bandage-conservative management
2. Internal splinting - k wire, plates, screws - surgical management
3. Continuous traction – is a method of immobilization. It's useful in hip dislocation, cervical injury and shaft of femur fracture.

Rules of bandaging

1. Correct size of bandage must be assessed according to the part to be covered

1 inch width	fingers and toes
2 inch width	head
4 inch width	limbs
6 inch width	trunk

2. The part to be bandaged is kept in functional position before bandage.

elbow	ninety degree flexed position
ankle	dorsiflexed
metacarpophalangeal joint injuries	james' position
shoulder	mild abduction
colles' fracture	mild palmar flexion and ulnar deviation
knee	5-20 degree flexion

3. Head of bandage should be always on the outer aspect of the bandage
4. Turns should be taken from within outwards, i.e medial to lateral (charaka explained 2 types of bandages in charaka chikitsa 25th chapter- vama and dakshina)
5. Bandage is first fixed by taking 2 turns at the same level to prevent slipping
6. Equal pressure should be maintained throughout the bandage
7. A thick pad of cotton wool is applied for giving tight bandage to prevent bleeding.
8. Each succeeding turn should overlap 2/3rd of preceding turn
9. 2 skin surfaces should not be bandaged together, keep a cotton piece covered with gauze in buddy strapping, if 2 fingers are bandaged together
10. All dressing must be covered properly
11. Tip of fingers and toes should be exposed to assess the circulation and movement, to check capillary refilling test at end of bandage

Signs of tight bandage

1. Blue tinge to the fingernail/toenail
2. Blue or pale skin color
3. Tingling or loss of sensation
4. Coldness of the extremity
5. Inability to move the fingers/toes

Rules of rebandage

1. soumya rithu - 7 days
2. Sadharana (madhyama) - 5 days (sarath, vasantha ritu as tika of vagbhata, A.H SU 27)
3. Agneyam   - 3 days

Bandage at various parts

- For toe - 2 circular turns around ankle, make turn around foot passing over the dorsum and across the sole to reach inner side of toe, then spiral turns, again back to the leg retained by circular turns
- Foot - 2 circular turns made at lower part of foot, take spiral turns up to balls of toe, take reversed spiral turns to the lower part of leg
- Ankle and heel - divergent spica is used, firstly around ankle circular turns, bandage rolled upwards and downwards to make divergent spica
- Leg - spiral turns (anuvelita bandha)
- Knee - in 5-20 degree flexion position - figure of 8 (swasthika bandha)
- Thigh - spiral and reversed spiral is used
- Groin - spica (swasthika bandha) is used, starting from upper part of thigh, 2 -3 spiral turns round thigh from within outward
- Perineum and anus - t bandage (gophana bandha) is used, horizontal bandage around waist, vertical limb will hang from the posterior part, then it is brought forward between thigh over the anus then tied separately to horizontal limb
- Abdomen and thorax- many tailed bandage (vibandha bandha)
- Fracture of clavicle - figure of 8 (swasthika bandha) applied in front of shoulder round axilla and crossing at the back
- Lower jaw and TMJ - 4 tailed bandage (khatva) and 5 tailed bandage (panchangi)

Susrutha Acharya explained 14 bandha visesha.

कोशदामस्वस्तिकानुवेल्लितमु(प्र)तोलीमण्डलस्थगिकायमकखट्वाचीनविबन्धवितानगोफणाः पञ्चाङ्गी चेति चतुर्दश बन्धविशेषाः (SU SU 18)

तत्र कोशमङ्गुष्ठाङ्गुलिपर्वसु विदध्यात्, दाम सम्बाधेऽङ्गे, सन्धिकूर्चकभ्रूस्तनान्तरतलकर्णेषु स्वस्तिकं, अनुवेल्लितं शाखासु, ग्रीवामेढ्रयोः मु(प्र)तोलीं, वृत्तेऽङ्गे मण्डलम्, अङ्गुष्ठाङ्गुलिमेढ्राग्रेषु स्थगिकां, यमलव्रणयोर्यमकं, हनुशङ्खगण्डेषु खट्वाम्, अपाङ्गयोश्चीनं, पृष्ठोदरोरःसु विबन्धं, मूर्धनि वितानं, चिबुकनासौष्ठांसबस्तिषु गोफणां, जत्रुण ऊर्ध्वं पञ्चाङ्गीमिति (SU SU 18)

Vagbhata Acharya explained 15 bandha visesha.

कोशदामोत्सङ्गस्वस्तिकानुवेल्लितमुत्तोलीमण्डलस्थविकायमकखट्वाचीनविबन्ध

वितानगोष्फणाः पञ्चाङ्गी

चेति पञ्चदश बन्धविशेषाः।

तत्र कोशमङ्गुलीपर्वसु विदध्यात्।

दाम सम्बाधेऽङ्गे।

उत्सङ्ग विलम्बिनि।

स्वस्तिकं सन्धि कूर्चभ्रूस्तनान्तरकुक्ष्यक्षिकपोलकर्णेषु।

अनुवेल्लितं शाखासु।

मुत्तोलीं ग्रीवामेढ्रयोः।

मण्डलं वृत्तेऽङ्गे।

स्थविकामङ्गुष्ठाङ्गमेढ्राग्रामूत्रवृद्धिषु।

यमकं यमलव्रणयोः।

ख़ट्वां हनुशङ्खगण्डेषु।

चीनमपाङ्गयोः।

विबन्धमुदरोरुपृष्ठेषु।

वितानं मूर्धादौ पृथुलेऽङ्गे।

गोष्फणंनासौष्ठचिबुकसन्धिषु।

पञ्चाङ्गी जत्रूर्ध्वमिति। (AS SU 38)

Tika of utsangi

उत्सङ्गमुत्सङ्गमिव विलम्बिनि बाह्वादौ कण्ठादिलम्बमानम् (शशिलेक व्याख्या (इन्दु कृत))

Utsangi is added as the fifteenth bandha by Vagbhata Acharya. It's a sling or triangular bandage highly useful in upper limb injuries.

Clinical application of bandha

• Colles' fracture	• anuvellita (spiral bandage) + utsangi (sling or triangular bandage)
• Shoulder dislocation	• swastika (shoulder spica) + utsangi
• Tibia and fibula distal end fracture	• anuvellita (spiral bandage)

• Interphalangeal dislocation	• kosha (sheath bandage)
• Hip joint • Bilateral avascular necrosis	• dama (loose bandage)
• Rib fracture	• vibandha (many tailed bandage)
• T12 wedge compression fracture	• vibandha
• Ankle sprain	• swasthika (divergent spica)
• Grade I knee ligament sprain knee and ankle	• swasthika (figure of eight bandage)
• Perianal region • after ksharakarma, kshara sutra	• gophana bandha (T bandage)
• Temporomandibular(TMJ) dislocation	• khatva (four tailed bandage) or panchangi (five tailed bandage)
• Head injury without raised IntraCranial Tension	• vithana (cephalic bandage)
• Pindi in eye	• cheena (eye bandage)
• Acute low back pain	• swasthika (hip spica)
• Clavicle fracture	• swastika (figure of eight)

Clinical application of Orthosis

• Shoulder dislocation	• shoulder immobilizer
• Recurrent shoulder dislocation	• shoulder support (only during activities)
• Acute knee injury grade II ligament sprain	• knee immobilizer
• Acute knee injury grade I ligament sprain	• knee brace
• Grade I lateral collateral ligament (ATFL) ligament sprain of ankle	• ankle binder
• T12 wedge compression fracture	• thoracolumbosacral corset (TLSO)
• Rib fracture	• rib belt
• Mallet finger	• mallet splint
• Clavicle fracture	• clavicle brace or figure of eight
• Ulnar collateral ligament sprain	• thumb spica splint
• Finger fracture and dislocation	• finger cot
• Lateral epicondylitis	• tennis elbow band
• Carpal tunnel syndrome	• wrist splint
• De-quervain's tenosynovitis	• thumb spica splint
• Trigger finger	• finger extension splint
• Iliotibial band syndrome	• Iliotibial band support
• Osgood schlatter disease	• patellar strap
• Posterior tibial tendonitis	• custom arch support

Internal medication protocol in acute injury

1. Mustadi marma kashaya
2. Punarnavadi kashaya
3. Manjishtadi kashaya
4. Rasnerandadi kashaya
5. Dhanwantaram kashaya (subacute or chronic injury)

If it's a chronic injury, it's recommended to use Dhanwantaram kashaya and Laksha guggulu in the first phase.

In the second phase, occurring within 2 to 6 weeks of the injury in acute cases, the use of Gandha Tailam along with Lakshadi Choorna with Ksheera is recommended. Sudha Laksha Choorna can also be employed for the same purpose during this phase. Additionally, internally, Dhanwantaram Kashaya, along with Kaisoraguggulu and Dhanwantaram Taila Avarthy, is administered at this stage.

In the last phase, when rehabilitation begins, internal sneha prayoga is implemented based on Agnibala. For this purpose, Dhanwantaram Taila, Bala Taila, Sahacharadi Taila, Rasnadasamooladi Ghrita, and Gugguluthiktaka Ghrita are utilized. These internal applications aim to support the rehabilitation process and promote healing, following the principles of Ayurveda.

In all upper limb and lower limb injury after the initial management of fracture, as bhagna anubandha or bhagnananthara chikitsa, prasakha anuvasana is mentioned by Acharya Sushruta. So it's better to do anuvasana vasti at the time of rehabilitation to get the functional movements earlier. Dhanwantaram taila, bala taila, sahacharadi taila are recommended for the same.

प्रशाखास्वनुवासनम् (SU.CHI 3)

These three methods can be employed in cases with **delayed healing**, which are found to be highly effective.

1. **Asthi shrinkhala bhavitha Aabha guggulu** is advisable to use internally for better healing of fractures.
2. **Laksha, madhuka and lasuna** (in chakradatta bhagnadhikara) are used as ksheera kashaya. It can also be used along with the gandha taila in the cellular proliferation stage. The amount taken is 1 karsha.
3. Following prayoga explained by Susrutha, **grushti ksheera** (prepared with madhuroushada gana, kakolyadi) with **laksha** can be incorporated.

गृष्टिक्षीरं ससर्पिष्कं मधुरौषधसाधितम् ॥१३॥

शीतलं लाक्षया युक्तं प्रातर्भग्नः पिबेन्नरः (SU.CHI 3)

Dalhana tika

गृष्टिः प्रथमप्रसूता गौः। कल्पना चेयं- काकोल्यादीनां मधुराणां कर्षमात्रं द्रव्यमष्टगुणं क्षीरं चतुर्गुणोदकसिद्धं क्षीरशेषं सर्पिर्लाक्षाकर्षमात्रप्रक्षेपान्वितं (SU.CHI 3)

Laksha- 1 karsha- 12 g

Pathya of bhagna

शालिमांसरसः क्षीरं सर्पिर्यूषः सतीनजः।

बृंहणं चान्नपानं स्यादद्येयं भग्नाय जानता (SU.CHI 3)

Apathya of bhagna

लवणं कटुकं क्षारमम्लं मैथुनमातपम्।

व्यायामं च न सेवेत भग्नो रूक्षान्नमेव च (SU.CHI 3)

To ensure healing of fracture, it's advisable to check clinically

- Absence of tenderness
- Regained movements
- Presence of transmitted movements

भग्नं सन्धिमनाविद्धमहीनाङ्गमनुल्बणम्।

सुखचेष्टप्रचारं च संहितंसम्यगादिशेत् (SU.CHI 3)

Radiologically, callus formation and formation of normal bony trabeculae suggests healing of fracture.

MANAGEMENT PROTOCOL OF PATHOLOGICAL CONDITIONS (COLD ORTHOPEDICS)

1. **Ama pachana and sopha hara**
2. **Transitional phase**
3. **Internal sneha –samana or brumhana**
4. **Rasayana**
5. **Rehabilitation - starting after ama pachana**

1. **The first treatment protocol is ama pachana and sophahara.**

If there's intense pain, severe tenderness with morning stiffness lasting for more time, pain at night with discomfort, it can be considered as a pittavruta vata condition. For this, a better option to adopt is ama pachana drugs explained in pitta jwara chikitsa, Amruthotharam or Pachanamrutham. For kaphavruta vata conditions, in which there will be more swelling and heaviness, Danadanayanadi or Dasamoola and Rasnapanchakam would be the appropriate choices.

In all Ashtavaidya traditional treatment protocols, the morning kashaya is for anulomana, and the evening kashaya is for samana of the disease. This approach is beneficial in musculoskeletal pathological conditions. For example, in a kaphavruta vata situation, Gandharva Hasthadi is advisable to administer in the morning, and Danadanayanadi in the evening.

Application of rookshavasthi with pachanamruta kashaya 300ml, vasiwnara choorna 30 g and saindhava 15 g, is a better option to be administered as an op procedure for quick ama pachana.

2. **In the transitional phase, based on condition, it's advisable to opt for :**
a. **Eranda**
b. **Ksheera kashaya**
c. **Taila, Ghrita in kashaya**

When a patient reports morning stiffness and pain at night, it's recommended to focus on ama pachana and sopha hara treatment. When patients' mention that the morning stiffness has eased but now experience exertional or mechanical pain, it's better to make the transition to the next phase. Rehabilitation should commence only after ama pachana to avoid aggravation of pain and symptoms.

For **Pitta Kopa** Condition:

- **Nimbamritadi Eranda** can be used. It is recommended to take five drops of Nimbamritadi Eranda twice daily. **Yashti choorna** (1 tsp) can be added.

For **Kapha Kopa** Condition:

- Sindhuvara Eranda is suggested. Additionally, **Triphala choorna** (1 tsp) can be added. The dosage is twice daily.

3. **In the third phase, it's better to start internal sneha**

For internal sneha, as snayu, sandhi, and sira of madhyama rogamarga are affected in pathological conditions of musculoskeletal diseases, it's better to adopt taila or mahasneha internally. It's a kevala vata situation after the first 2 phases. For the same, it's possible to utilise Dhanwantharam taila **(more effective for motor weakness and white matter pathology, proximal muscle weakness)**, Ksheerabala taila **(more effective for sensory** issues, grey matter pathology, distal muscle weakness), Karpasasthyadi taila (more effective for upper trunk, cervical and upper limb issues), Bala taila (for degenerative diseases, cartilage strengthening), Sahacharadi taila (neurovascular issues).

While selecting ghrita, either Rasnadasamooladi ghrita or Thikta Rasa Ghrita like Thiktaka, Mahathiktaka or Gugguluthiktaka ghrita is advisable.

Another criterion that can be followed for internal samana snehapana is, in **inflammatory diseases, after ama pachana, ghrita is a better option and it's better to use taila in degenerative diseases.**

The dose of internal sneha should be based on the agnibala of the patient. **It's advisable to take internal Sneha in a large quantity (eg:- 10-20 ml) for a small period (2-3 weeks) than a small quantity (5 ml) for a large period(8 weeks).**

It's recommended to give it as shamana sneha or brumhana sneha. **The patient should take shamana sneha or brumhana sneha only at the time of appetite**. And next time, when the patient feels appetite after snehapana, it's possible to take food in samana snehapana.

4. Rasayana prayoga

Selection of Rasayana depends on the structure or dhatu affected. If it's the bone or its sub-tissue (upadhatu), it's better to prescribe **Gandha Tailam** (10 drops) for 2–3 months or Krishna Tila (5 gm) with Amalaki Choorna (5 g) in hot water for the same period. **Sudha laksha choorna** shall be administered as ksheera kashaya for the same purpose. If the muscle tissue is affected, **Kaisora Guggulu or Laksha Guggulu** is better advised for 2-3 months. For this, soak Kaisora Guggulu in Triphala kwatha overnight, and in the early morning, take 1 or 2 tablets, as guggulu absorption is better when soaked in Triphala kwatha.

Mamsa rasa with Asthi and Majja, can be incorporated for situations affecting the Asthi. Specifically, Mamsa Rasa with Mamsa can be administered when ligaments, tendons, fascia, and bursa are affected. The processing of these substances can be done with Kashaya medicines. Laksha can be added to enhance the therapeutic effects.

Additionally, the Ayurvedic formulation Chukkilirattyadi is mentioned as a potent Rasayana combination for strengthening Asthi Dhatu and its Upadhatu.

5. Rehabilitation

Rehabilitation needs to be personalized for each individual based on their specific needs and the nature of their disease or injury. It's crucial to ensure that patients do not experience pain during and after the rehabilitation process.

NOTE:

Internal Sneha, Rasayana, and Rehabilitation are the three most important factors that help us to provide Sudha Chikitsa (complete cure without recurrence).

In a patient with grade 4 osteoarthritis, (who is not willing for TKR due to comorbidities or financial issues) which is a yapya disease, ask the patient to come for a follow-up in a gap of 3 months or 6 months. After assessing the agnibala of the patient, either advise the patient to do virechana after sadyasneha and give internal sneha for a period of 2 weeks, or if the patient is reluctant to take internal sneha, it's advisable to do the matravasti with Dhanwantharam Taila for 14 days. It will help the patient maintain the result obtained by the above mentioned management protocol.

The approach for managing chronic pathologies and fibromyalgia, incorporating Virechana with Agasthyar kuzhampu preceding it with Sadyovamana using Yashti kashaya. This protocol aims to not only address the immediate symptoms but also reduce the recurrence and provide sustained relief.

- Sadyovamana Prior to Virechana:
- Sadyovamana, is advised before Virechana. Yashti kashaya shall be used for Sadyovamana.
- Virechana with Agasthyar Kuzhampu (100 mg in a gap of 6 months):
- Virechana, is suggested using Agasthyar kuzhambu, 100 mg at 6 am in the morning. This is recommended every 6 months to manage chronic pathologies and fibromyalgia.

This sequential approach is aimed at reducing recurrence and prolonging the relief achieved through the protocol.

Sports injury - Repetitive strain injury (RSI)

In a sports person, the need for the ama pachana stage will be minimal compared to other patients. A modified approach considering ama, dhatu, and poshana shall be incorporated. The concept to be followed includes:

- **Marma kshata chikitsa -rookshana and vasthi (CH.SI 9)**
- Bhagna chikitsa
- **Snayu Sandhigata vata chikitsa**
- Uthana vatarakta chikitsa
- **Dhara (seka)** – dhanyamla, kashaya, ksheera kashaya, taila is advisable in the order
- **Lepa** – nagaradi, ellumnisadi, gruhadoomadi are found to be effective
- **Rasayana** and nutritional support
- Understanding biomechanics, kinesiology and **sports psychology**
- Selective orthosis for sports events before complete recovery
- Incorporation of **Anusastra** on indicated situations
- Implementation of manual therapies, trigger point release, myofascial release, kinesio taping with the help of a **qualified physiotherapist** without compromising our concepts.

- Yoga and pranayama to maintain confidence

MARMA KSHATA CHIKITSA

विश्लिष्टदेहं पतितं मथितं हतमेव च ॥७७॥

वासयेत्तैलपूर्णायां द्रोण्यां मांसरसाशनम् |

अयमेव विधिः कार्यः क्षीणे मर्महते तथा (SU CHI 2)

SNAYU SANDHIGATA VATA CHIKITSA

स्नावसन्धिशिराप्राप्ते स्नेहदाहोपनाहनम् (A.H CHI 21)

NOTE:

Integration and teamwork will surely be fruitful in sports patient management for better outcome.

SPECIAL PROCEDURES - ANUSASTRA

SIRAVEDHA

A procedure to immediately relieve pain is siravedha. In Gridhrasi, Acharya explains **Antara Kandara gulphayaoranthare**. In viswachi, it's **kshiprasya dwayangulo upari**. Just before 48 minutes (1 muhurtha), give the patient sadyasneha and then perform siraveda using a **No. 18 needle** (an improvisation of **vreehimukha sastra**- mamsala pradesha siravedanartha) from the advised site. Immediately after the procedure, 50-80% relief will be present in 95% of cases.

लाघवं वेदनाशान्तिर्व्याघेर्वेगपरिक्षयः |

सम्यग्विस्राविते लिङ्गं प्रसादो मनसस्तथा (SU SU 14)

Manaprasada is seen only after raktamoksha, and it's possible to observe it on the patient's face. The relief can be explained with the concept of raktavruta vataprakopa chikitsa. In diseases affected with rakta involvement, treatment explained in Charaka Sutra 24, Vidhisoniteeyam chapter is,

1. Vireka
2. Upavasa
3. Raktapittaharikriya
4. Raktamoksha

In raktavruta vata prakopa lakshana, there is sparsadwesha or tvak mamsantharayo ruja.

रक्तावृते सदाहार्तिस्त्वङ्मांसान्तरजो भृशम्॥

भवेत् सरागः श्वयथुर्जायन्ते मण्डलानि च (CH CHI 28)

सूचीभिरिव निस्तोदः स्पर्शद्वेषः प्रसुप्तता ॥

शेषाः पित्तविकाराः स्युर्मारुते शोणितान्विते । (SU NI 1)

Apart from this, sparsadwesa as a lakshana is only seen in injury, i.e., fracture or dislocation. In both these conditions, raktamoksha is contraindicated. Whenever there is sparshadwesa in pathological conditions, it's advisable to employ raktamoksha considering it as raktavruta vataprakopa, to get rid of avarana and for the proper channelisation of vayu anuloma gati.

NB. Phlebotomy is the treatment of choice for hemochromatosis, polycythemia vera, sickle cell disease, and nonalcoholic fatty liver disease with hyperferritinemia.

The preoperative procedure for siraveda is sadya sneha. It is administered before 48 minutes (1 muhurta) of the main procedure. Post-operatively, the protection of agni and vayu of this particular patient is important. Give a solute replacement therapy immediately (first glass of water with sugar or salt and rest normal water) after the procedure and ask the patient to take food at the correct interval based on agni. Also, remember that all anusastra procedures can be done once, but if needed, it can be repeated in a gap of 14 days or 28 days, once more.

अशुद्धन्तु रक्तमपराह्णेऽन्येद्युर्वा पुनः स्रावयेत्।

ततोऽपि शेषं सर्वथा वाप्यविस्रावव्यक्तस्य शीतसेकप्रदेहविरेकोपवासस्निग्धमधुरान्नपानैः प्रसादयेत्।

मासमात्रं वा स्नेहादिभिरुपचर्य पुनर्विध्येत् (A.H SU 36)

Conducting thorough clinical examinations before and after anusastra procedures is essential. This approach ensures proper assessment, documentation of symptom relief, and overall effectiveness of the treatment.

Before proceeding with the procedure, it's important to conduct basic blood investigations and check for viral markers such as HIV, HBV, and HCV.

Additionally, assessing whether the patient is taking anticoagulants is crucial. If anticoagulants are in use, it's advisable to ask the patient to discontinue them for 2 days before the procedure. If a patient is on warfarin, siraveda must be contraindicated, as bleeding cannot be arrested. Also, ask if the patient has any kind of congenital disorders, like hemophilia, prior to procedure.

Clinical application and Indications

Siraveda shall be done from **kshiprasya dvungala upari (foot)** for these conditions

- Plantar fasciitis

- Retrocalcaneal bursitis (RCB)
- Achilles tendonitis
- Peroneal tendonitis
- Tibialis posterior tenosynovitis
- Tarsal tunnel syndrome (TTS)

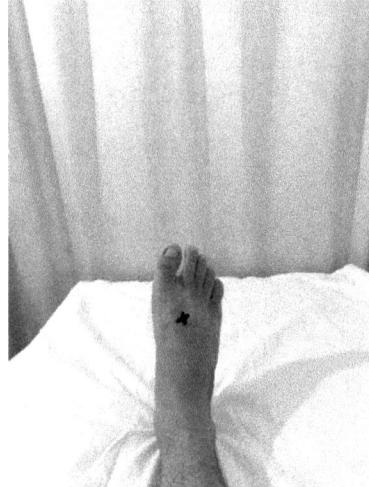

Kshiprasya dwayangula upari

Siraveda from **anthara kandara gulphayoranthare** (posterior tibial vein) is effective in

- L4-L5, L5-S1, L1-L2, L2-L3, L3-L4 radiculopathy
- Venous pooling due to varicose vein
- Severe mono articular ankle pain in a rheumatoid arthritis patient

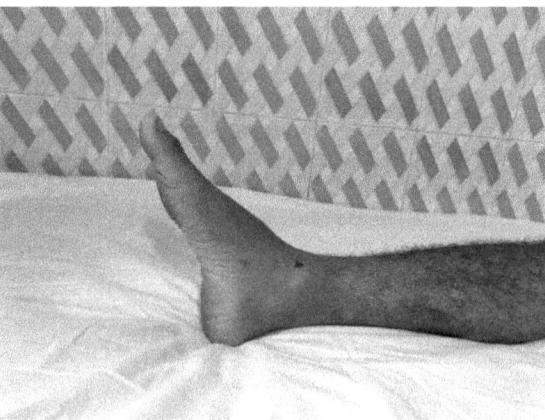

Anthara kandara gulphayoranthare

Siraveda shall be done from **kshiprasya dvungala upari (hand)** for these conditions

- C6-C7, C8-T1 cervical radiculopathy
- Carpal tunnel syndrome (CTS)
- De-quervain's tenosynovitis

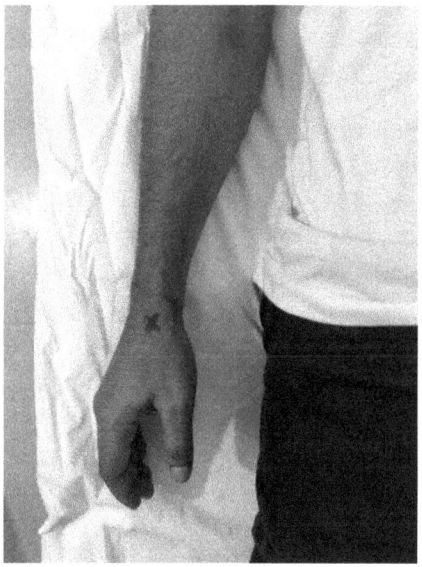

kshiprasya dvungala upari (hand)

Siraveda from the **koorpara sandhi** is effective in

- C4-C5, C5-C6 radiculopathy
- Supraspinatus tendonitis, biceps tendonitis, subacromial bursitis
- First stage of adhesive capsulitis

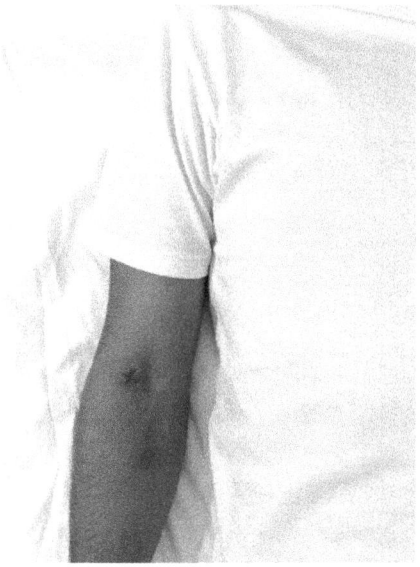

NOTE:

Siraveda is only effective in the first stage of adhesive capsulitis. It will reduce pain and bring about a change in Range Of Movements. In the second stage, there won't be any change in ROM and symptoms. Initially, in adhesive capsulitis, there is margavarana or srothorodha, which responds to siraveda. In the later phase of capsulitis, there is dhatu kshaya, in which siraveda is contraindicated.

Acharya Susrutha is explaining another site, 4 Angula above and 4 Angula below janu in lumbar radiculopathy. As an explanation, in upper lumbar radiculopathy raktamoksha can be done from 4 angula above janu, and in lower lumbar radiculopathy raktamoksha can be done from 4 angula below janu. But better to follow siraveda from **Anthara kandara gulphayoranthare** for both upper and lower lumbar radiculoapthy and it's found effective in both situations.

Regarding the selection of raktamoksha, it's better to employ this criterion.

- For a single tender point - alabu/srunga
- For action needed at an area of 1 hasta (24A) - jalooka
- Above 1 hasta, one limb is affected or whole body - siraveda

अवगाढे जलौका स्यात् प्रच्छनं पिण्डिते हितम् |

सिराऽङ्गव्यापके रक्ते शृङ्गालाबू त्वचि स्थिते (SU SA 8)

AGNIKARMA

In all soft tissue injuries like lateral and medial epicondylitis, supraspinatus tendonitis, plantar fasciitis, iliotibial band syndrome (ITBS), retrocalcaneal bursitis (RCB), due to repetitive strain injury (RSI), agnikarma can be done if the pain is not well responded in 2-3 weeks of ama pachana, sopha hara medicine internally.

It's better to do agnikarma after upanaha over the affected site for 3 days, with ellumnisadi or gruhadoomadi or nagaradi as the cause is RSI. After agnikarma, internal sneha should be given.

स्नावसन्धिशिराप्राप्ते स्नेहदाहोपनाहनम् (A.H CHI 21)

Rooksha agnikarma with salaka is preferable in soft tissue injuries. In spinal conditions and chronic conditions, snigdha agnikarma with madhu (honey) or taila is better.

पिप्पल्यजाशकृद्दोदन्तशरशलाकास्त्वग्गतानां, जाम्बवौष्ठेतरलौहा मांसगतानां, क्षौद्रगुडस्नेहाः सिरास्नायुसन्ध्यस्थिगतानाम् (SU SU 12)

अग्निसन्तप्तो हि स्नेहः सूक्ष्मसिरानुसारित्वात्त्वगादीननुप्रविश्याशु दहति (SU SU 12)

SUMMARY OF ANUSASTRA

Meticulous care should be taken for preoperative and postoperative protocols in anusastra. In pitta prakopa conditions, agnikarma is contraindicated. In such situations, raktamoksha is advisable.

Agnikarma on a single sitting will lead to ama pachana over the site. The action of Agnikarma can be explained with the help of **heat shock proteins (HSP)**. Heat shock proteins are activated by heat and reduce local inflammation, having an immunomodulatory effect.

Clinically, Agnikarma provides symptomatic relief, and raktamoksha provides symptomatic relief as well as reversal of pathology. It relieves raktavruta vata prakopa. As it's a sodhana procedure, the force of elimination has a role in better results. The amount of blood is not a factor for relief of symptoms. It's advised to take a maximum up to 1 prastha (around 650 ml maximum, 1 prastha = 16 pala, but in sodhana, it's 13.5 pala). Around 100 ml-350 ml surely gives relief around 50-80% in a single sitting. After the first sitting, if needed (not needed in all cases), siraveda shall be repeated after 15 days or 1 month, and the next sitting should be done only after 6 months.

ANUSASTRA

deep seated, more pittadika	JALOOKA
A single point, kaphadika	ALABU/ MODIFIED SRUNGA
1 limb is affected or whole body	SIRAVEDA
Soft tissue pathology with kaphadika	ROOKSHA AGNIKARMA
Soft tissue pathology with vatadika	SNIGDHA AGNIKARMA
Soft tissue pathology with pittadika	JALOOKA

AVAGAHA SWEDA

Another highly beneficial procedure like raktamoksha is **avagaha sweda**. In lumbar radiculopathy conditions, it's better to do avagaha sweda for a time of 5 min to 10 min in sukoshna jala prepared with any vatahara dravya and saindhava. While doing the procedure, the patient should be given ample support to sit. It should be done in a proper hip sitz bath container where the patient should completely sit. The patient should rise from the tub with the support of two other people. Look for the samyak swinna lakshna i.e. sweda appears in the nose. At that time, stop avagaha. If Avagaha sweda is done for 20 min, i.e. atiyoga, then pain will aggravate in lumbar radiculopathy conditions.

4. SHOULDER JOINT

APPLIED ANATOMY OF SHOULDER JOINT

Shoulder joint consists of articulations:

1. Glenohumeral joint: The true glenohumeral joint is the articulation between the glenoid cavity of the scapula and the head of the humerus.

   The head of the humerus has one-third apposition with the glenoid cavity. The glenoid cavity is shallow and is deepened by the glenoid labrum.

2. Sternoclavicular joint
3. Acromioclavicular joint.
4. Scapulothoracic joint - physiological joint with no synovial cavity

The sternoclavicular, acromioclavicular, and scapulothoracic joints functionally help the shoulder joint attain the complete ROM.

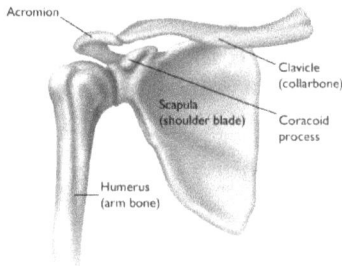

Rotator cuff muscles / musculotendinous cuff

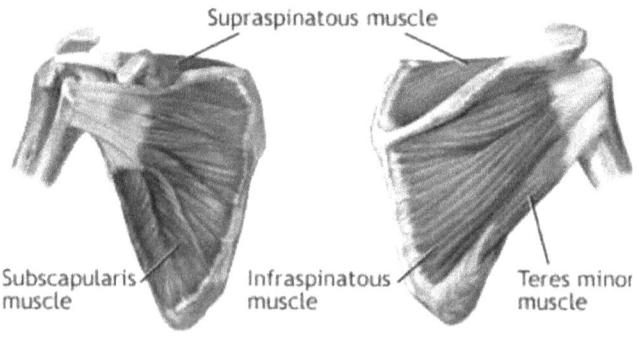

Are 4 muscles

1. Supraspinatus

2. Infraspinatus

3. Teres minor

4 Subscapularis.

* In this the subscapularis muscle is attached anteriorly and it facilitates medial rotation of the shoulder joint.

* The supraspinatus muscle is connected superiorly and it helps the initial abduction of the shoulder and the Deltoid muscle helps in further Abduction. Out of 180-degree abduction, 120 degrees is by glenohumeral joint and 60 degrees is by rotation of the scapula.

• Posteriorly infraspinatus and teres minor are seen which helps in the external rotation of shoulder joint.

CLINICAL EXAMINATION-ROTATOR CUFF MUSCLES

* To check the patency of the supraspinatus muscle ask the patient to abduct the shoulder. If the patient shrugs the shoulder for initiation of abduction, the patient's supraspinatus muscle is affected.

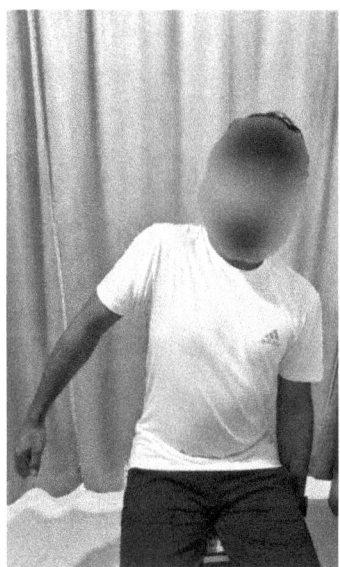

• The external rotation of the shoulder joint is restricted by the examiner. If the patient feels pain in the area of posterior axillary fold while doing this maneuver it gives inference that the infraspinatus and teres minor muscle are affected.

Gerber's lift-off test

The shoulder joint is in internal rotation and the examiner pushes the hand of the patient and the patient pushes the hand towards the examiner. This test is called Gerber's lift-off test. If the patient feels pain on the anterior side, then the subscapularis muscle is affected.

The ligaments of the shoulder joint

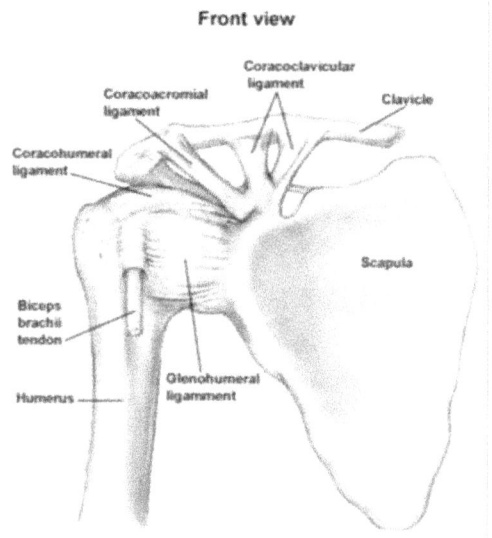

- Conoid ligament
- Trapezoid ligament

Both are also known as the Coracoclavicular ligament. These two ligaments are important when discussing acromioclavicular subluxation.

- Acromioclavicular ligament
- Coracoacromial ligament - prevents superior displacement of the head of the humerus
- Coracohumeral ligament
- Transverse humeral ligament
- Superior glenohumeral ligament
- Middle glenohumeral ligament
- Inferior glenohumeral ligament - attached to the glenoid capsule and gives more strength to the joint.

Stability of the Shoulder joint

1. Coracoacromial arch
2. Musculotendinous cuff /rotator cuff of the shoulder
3. Glenoid labrum - helps in deepening the glenoid fossa
4. Muscles attaching the humerus to the pectoral girdle

5. Long head of biceps.
6. Long head of triceps

Whenever planning rehabilitation to the shoulder joint for strengthening, it's better to focus on advising rehabilitation to all these structures which are providing stability to the shoulder.

RANGE OF MOTION

- Flexion -140°
- Extension - 45°
- Abduction - 180°
- Adduction - 0°
- Medial (internal) rotation - 90°
- Lateral (external) rotation - 90°
- Circumduction- combination of flexion, extension and adduction, abduction.

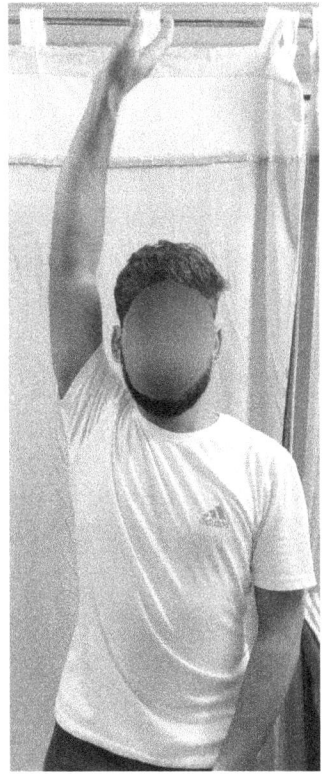

Abduction

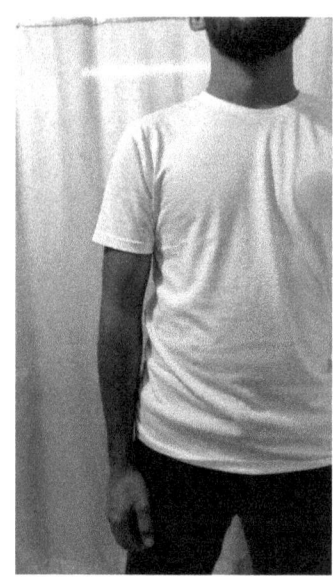

Adduction

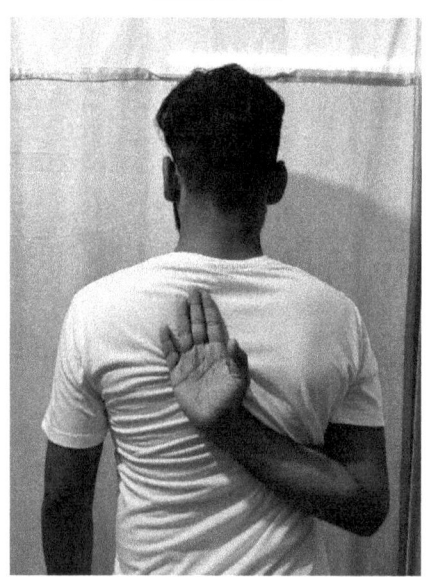

Internal rotation

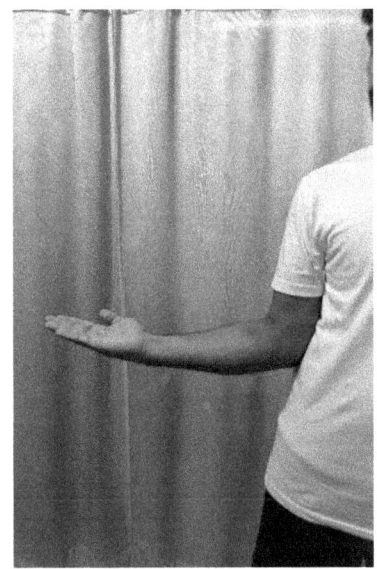

External rotation

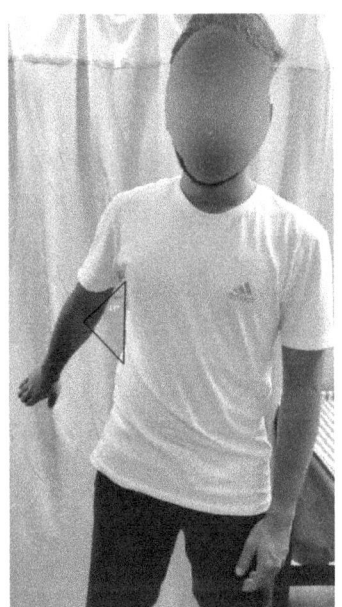

Extension

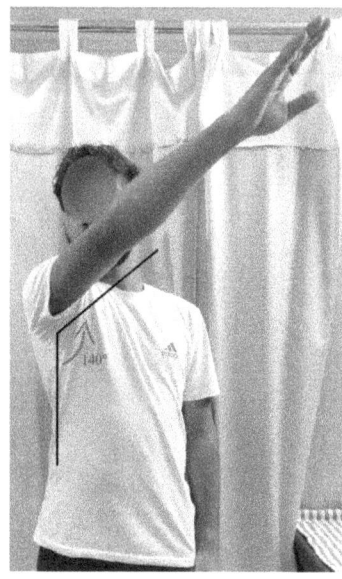

Flexion

When compared with the other joints, the shoulder joint has more mobility and less stability.

The glenoid cavity is 30° inclined to the horizontal plane so that Abduction is not on the complete horizontal plane, it is 30° inclined to the horizontal plane and the flexion is 90° to abduction so flexion is not directly forward it is 30° inclined to the forward plane.

The normal range of motion of flexion is 140° and just opposite to flexion is extension and the normal range is 45°.

The complete range of motion of abduction is 180°. If the patient feels difficulty with the initiation of abduction, then the supraspinatus muscle is affected.

The pain and discomfort in the 70° to 120° is due to painful arc syndrome.

If there is pain in the final 30° of abduction then it is due to acromioclavicular joint arthritis or due to acromioclavicular joint subluxation. So abduction itself gives more clues to the clinical diagnosis.

Just opposite to Abduction is Adduction.

Whenever we touch the opposite shoulder it is adducted across the chest. Medial rotation and lateral rotation are done in a 90° flexed elbow.

In the complete medial rotation, the patient can touch the opposite body of the scapula.

Another range of motion is external rotation and internal rotation in 90° abduction.

COMMON PATHOLOGIES OF SHOULDER JOINT

Each clinical situation shall be discussed in the form of a case presentation.

ADHESIVE CAPSULITIS

A 45-year-old female came to OPD with pain and a restricted range of motion in her shoulder. In the initial phase, she felt difficulty in washing, cleaning, and toweling the patient's backside ie; her posterior side. In the second phase, she felt difficulty in external rotation and abduction. After two to three weeks of pain in the movements, she started pain at night. She is unable to sleep due to pain while she rolls over and when she sleeps on the affected shoulder. X-ray of shoulder AP view is normal. The provisional diagnosis is Adhesive capsulitis. It's possible to ensure the diagnosis by checking Apley's scratch test.

In the initial phase, internal rotation is affected in Adhesive capsulitis or Periarthritis or Frozen shoulder.

Apley's scratch test

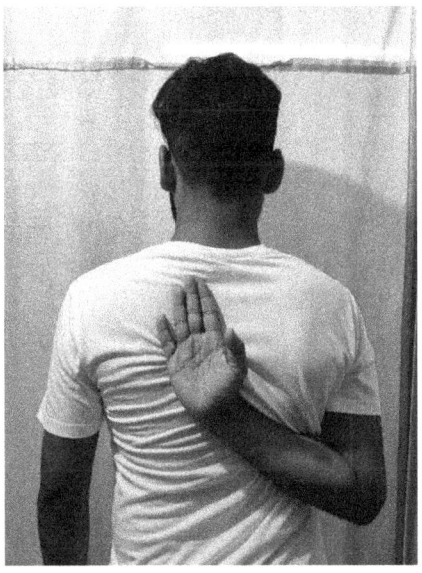

Internal rotation of right shoulder

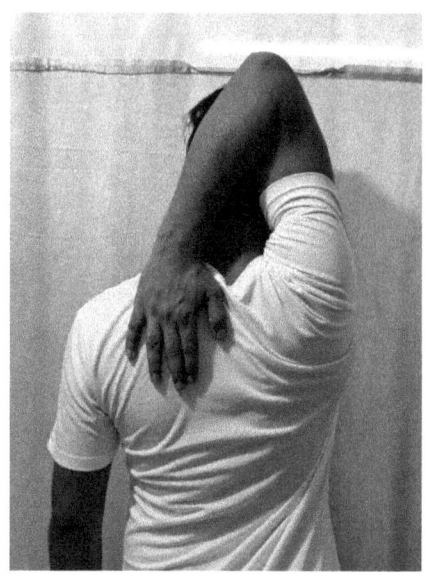

External rotation and abduction of right shoulder

It is the most common test to rule out whether the shoulder pain is due to cervical or shoulder pathology. The most common cause of shoulder pain is C 5 - C6 lesion. So whenever a patient comes with shoulder pain radiating down up to the mid arm, it's better to rule out whether it's cervical or shoulder. So Apley's test can be employed. One is internal rotation, another is external rotation and abduction simultaneously. If the patient is not having pain in Apley's scratch test then the cause is cervical pathology. It's possible to rule out apley's scratch in op within 10-20 seconds.

How to do apley's scratch test

- First step is to keep the shoulder in internal rotation.
- Next, the examiner should ask the patient to reach behind his head and touch the spine of the opposite scapula. This tests the abduction and external rotation movements.

Here, in this patient, the internal rotation, external rotation and abduction are restricted and it is due to adhesive capsulitis.

It's possible to do another test by holding the two hands together behind the head where external rotation and abduction are done. The affected shoulder can't be put in this position due to adhesive capsulitis.

In adhesive capsulitis, the internal rotation is first affected then external rotation and abduction are affected. A patient with adhesive capsulitis can't do internal rotation up to the medial border of the scapula, it falls much below the inferior angle. Some cases internal rotation is possible only up to the iliac crest. It's advisable to document internal rotation in each review to get an exact idea regarding relief of capsulitis.

It is more common in diabetic patients, but it may occur in patients without diabetes mellitus also. Adhesive capsulitis may also occur in post-traumatic situations, if rehabilitation is not employed at proper time.

Adhesive capsulitis includes a total of 3 stages.

- In the first phase, there is increasing pain.
- In the second phase, there is decreasing pain and increasing stiffness.
- And in the third phase, there is relief of both symptoms
- Each phase lasts for a total of 4 to 8 months.

In adhesive capsulitis, when the patient stops doing rehabilitation, then there will be restriction in range of motion of affected shoulder. We aim to preserve the range of motion while doing rehabilitation. Our primary aim is to reduce pain in the initial phase. The pathology is thickening and contracture of the joint capsule as seen in Dupuytren's contracture. In Dupuytren's contracture, there is thickness and contracture of palmar aponeurosis. In adhesive capsulitis there is thickening and contracture of the joint capsule covering the shoulder joint. It is prone to diabetes mellitus patients. It's better to do the rehabilitation as per guidelines for relief of adhesive capsulitis.

NOTE:

When a patient comes with unilateral shoulder pain, especially at night aged 55-60, please keep in mind the differential diagnosis of primary parkinsonism. Primary parkinsonism affects unilateral and most commonly upper limbs. Bradykinesia is the reason for adhesive capsulitis and shoulder pain. So proper management for primary parkinsonism is essential for the relief in such patients.

PAINFUL ARC SYNDROME

Coming to the next pathology, **painful arc syndrome** in which the pain is between 70° to 120° ie; pain in mid abduction. While doing abduction, the patient feels pain in 70° to 120° and on extreme abduction, there is absence of pain. Whenever the patient does adduction the pain reappears from 120° to 70°. In between 70° and 120° while doing abduction, if external rotation is done, then the pain disappears.

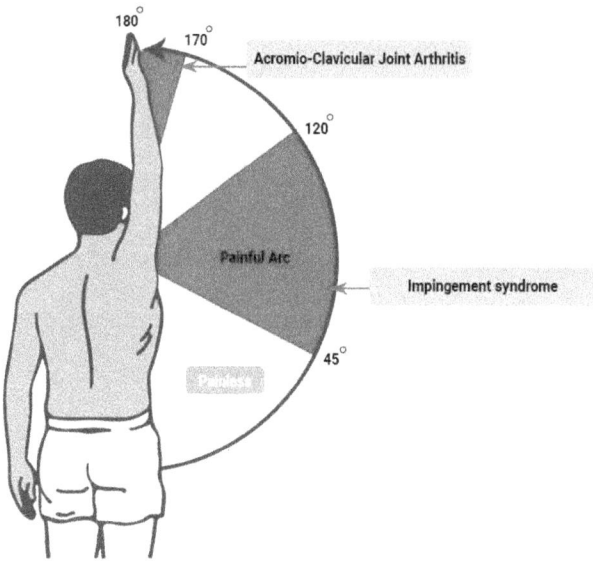

When the head of the humerus is in 70° to 120° abduction, there is less space between the acromion process and the head of the humerus. Whenever the subacromial bursa is swollen, and whenever the supraspinatus tendon is inflamed, there may be a chance of impingement and it causes pain. In this condition, the pain starts from the anterolateral aspect of the shoulder and radiates up to the mid arm.

There are 5 causes for painful arc syndrome which include

1. Supraspinatus tendonitis
2. Supraspinatus tendon tear
3. Calcified supraspinatus
4. Subacromial bursitis
5. Greater tuberosity fracture.

Among these causes, the greater tuberosity fracture and calcified supraspinatus can be differentially diagnosed by x-ray findings. In most cases, the greater tuberosity fractures occur due to avulsion ie, due to the pull of the supraspinatus muscle. The supraspinatus tendonitis shall be diagnosed by empty can test and the complete tear of supraspinatus tendon tear shall be diagnosed by drop arm test, empty can and full can test.

Empty can test

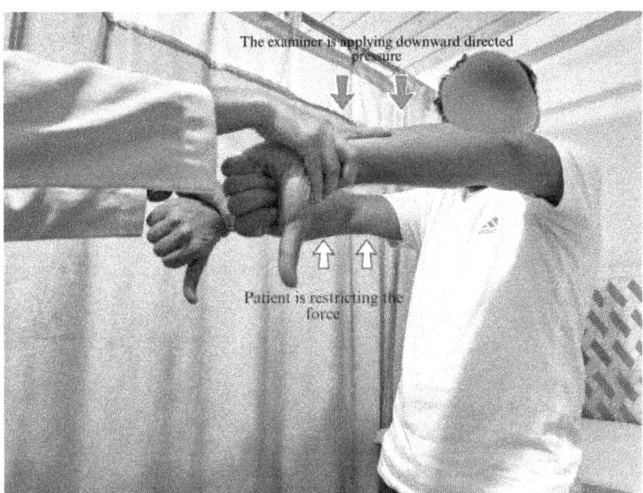

In an empty can test the patient's shoulder is in 90° abduction and internal rotation. The position resembles emptying of a can by keeping the shoulder in internal rotation, so that the name empty can test. Now ask the patient to abduct the shoulder in this position, that is in internal rotation. If there is supraspinatus tendonitis, the patient feels pain on the anterolateral aspect of the shoulder over the greater tuberosity where the supraspinatus tendon is inserted. Do this test on both the joints for comparison. A good practice involves conducting the clinical examination test initially on the normal or sound joint and subsequently on the affected joint.

BICEPS TENDONITIS

A case of a female patient aged 45 years. She felt pain mainly on the anterior shoulder while doing physical activities using her shoulder and elbow joint which included repeated flexion and extension of elbow and repeated adduction and abduction as part of her lifestyle. The provisional diagnosis is biceps tendonitis.

The long head of biceps is getting more painful in biceps tendonitis and pain is felt over the anterior part of the shoulder. In supraspinatus tendonitis, the pain is over the anterolateral aspect of the shoulder joint.

The pain pattern of biceps tendonitis

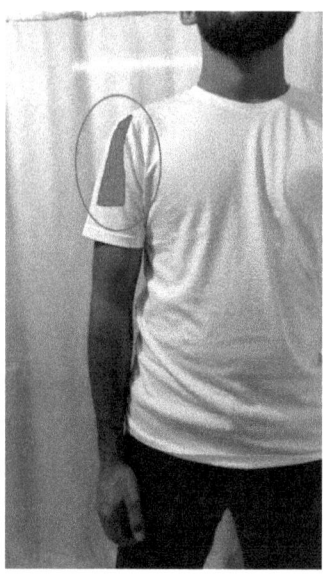

It's advisable to do the clinical examination, the speed test. Forward flexion or elevation of the shoulder against resistance causes pain anteriorly.

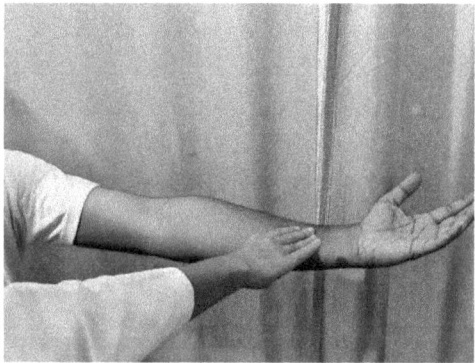

Speed test

AC JOINT ARTHRITIS

A male patient aged 50 years came to OPD who complained of pain on the final 30° of abduction. He has no pain on abduction up to 150° but the last 30° are painful and there is prominence and swelling of the Acromioclavicular Joint. On Palpation there is tenderness of acromioclavicular joint. The diagnosis is osteoarthritis of acromioclavicular joints. It is possible to confirm by crossed body adduction test.

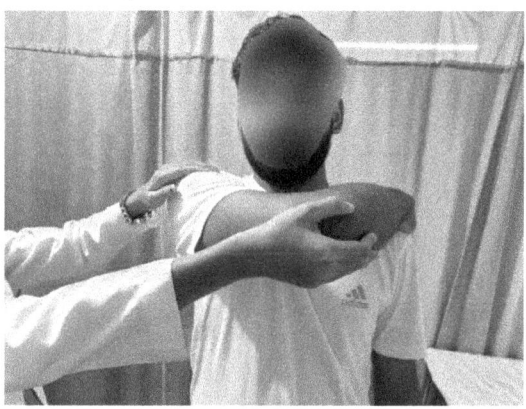

Crossed body adduction test

In the crossed-body adduction test the patient keeps the arm towards the opposite shoulder and the examiner does further adduction towards the chest by pushing to the opposite shoulder which causes typical pain in the acromioclavicular joint and is the confirmation of osteoarthritis of the acromioclavicular joint

The osteoarthritis of the glenohumeral joint is not much common when compared to the osteoarthritis of the acromioclavicular joint.

When there is osteoarthritis of the glenohumeral joint then the entire 180° abduction is painful. But in osteoarthritis of the acromioclavicular joint only the last 30° is painful and it's possible to diagnose it through the clinical examination, and crossed body adduction test.

In the OA glenohumeral joint, it's possible to visualise a **goat beard osteophyte** in the shoulder AP view X-ray

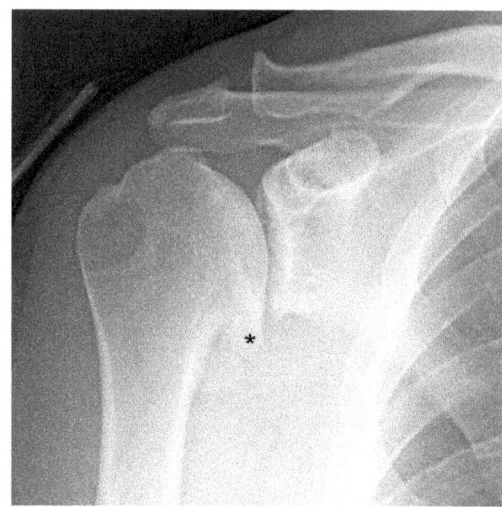

Management

In this particular disease, the initial management includes ama pachana and ama sophahara management.

In the second phase, the transition phase, and in the third phase, internal snehapana must be administered along with proper rehabilitation to facilitate and to strengthen the entire shoulder joint including the pectoral muscles, rotator cuff muscles, biceps, triceps and muscles over the posterior area connecting the scapula, spine and shoulder.

COMMON SHOULDER INJURY

SUPRASPINATUS TEAR

A 50-year-old male patient came to the OPD with a fall on an outstretched arm. There is severe pain in the shoulder immediately after the injury and the patient is unable to move the affected shoulder. The provisional diagnosis is supraspinatus tear.

The clinical examination includes the confirmatory test of supraspinatus tear which is a drop arm test.

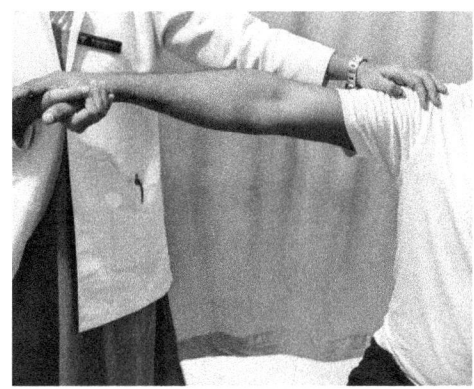 

The initial abduction of the shoulder joint is by the supraspinatus. In cases of complete tear of the supraspinatus, the patient is unable to do the abduction of the affected shoulder. But passively with the help of the examiner, patient can do abduction. In the drop arm test, passive abduction of the shoulder joint is done and when the examiner's hand is taken out, the arm drops down. It's a positive drop arm test, which is diagnostic of complete tear of supraspinatus. One of the actions of supraspinatus is initiation of abduction, second one is holding the arm in abduction (checking in drop arm), and third one prevents superior migration of head of the humerus. The complete supraspinatus tear causes superior migration of the head of the humerus. It is not dislocation or displacement. On X-ray shoulder, there will be superior migration of the head of the humerus in complete tear of supraspinatus.

If there is a partial tear of supraspinatus muscle then the patient can abduct his arm with pain. There will be tenderness on palpation of the tendon of the supraspinatus. When an empty can test is done and if there is pain at the insertion of supraspinatus, the test is positive, which is suggestive of partial tear of supraspinatus. Empty can tests will also be positive in supraspinatus tendonitis.

The management of partial tear of the supraspinatus muscle (acute injury) is either by giving a shoulder spica bandage or advice orthosis (shoulder immobilizer) for 3 weeks. After 3 weeks it's better to advise the patient to do the rehabilitation. Patients will be able to perform all the activities by 6 weeks of rehabilitation. If there is complete tear of the supraspinatus muscle, (diagnosed with drop arm, empty can and full can tests positive) refer the patient for surgical management. Complete tear shall always be ruled out clinically, by checking the drop arm test, empty can and full can tests.

CLAVICLE FRACTURE

The next case is a 17-year-old boy falling onto his shoulder and the patient is unable to move the affected shoulder. There is a visible deformity in the clavicle known as tenting. The clavicle is palpated from the sternoclavicular joint laterally towards the acromioclavicular joint with the examiner standing in the back of the patient. Whenever there is a fracture there is deformity. The most common fracture site is at the junction of the medial two-third and lateral one-third. Here the medial fragment of the clavicle moves upwards due to the pull of the sternocleidomastoid muscle and the lateral fragment moves downward due to the pull of pectoralis major.

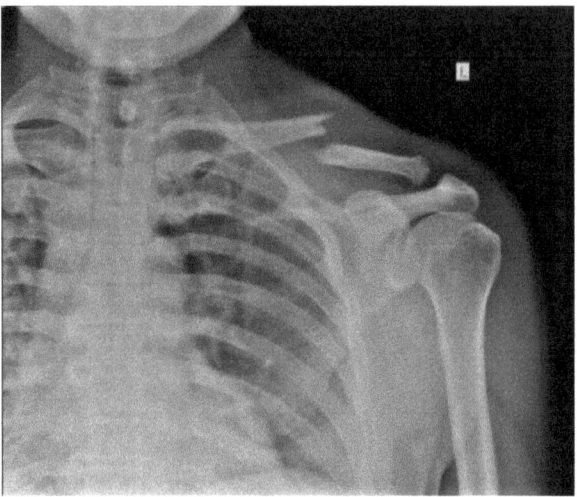

In this case, there is overlapping and the fracture won't unite.

To correct this misalignment Susrutha mentioned.

सन्नमुन्नमयेत् स्विन्नमक्षकं मुसलेन तु |

तथोन्नतं पीडयेच्च बध्नीयाद्दृढमेव च || (SU.CHI 3)

Which has gone down should be raised upwards and that which has gone upward should be placed down and Ghada Bandha is advised to avoid the redisplacement of the fragments due to the pull of muscles.

Here a figure of 8 bandage or clavicle brace is recommended. The expansion of the chest itself reduces the fracture. Whenever the chest expands both the fragments come into the correct apposition and for healing of fracture 50 percent apposition should be needed. It should be kept for 3 - 4 weeks. The clavicle brace should not be too tight. If it's too tight, there will be injury to the axillary artery, axillary nerve, and axillary vein. After 3-4 weeks, when the pain subsides, the affected shoulder and normal shoulder should be given continuous rehabilitation until the muscle strength and functional movements are completely regained.

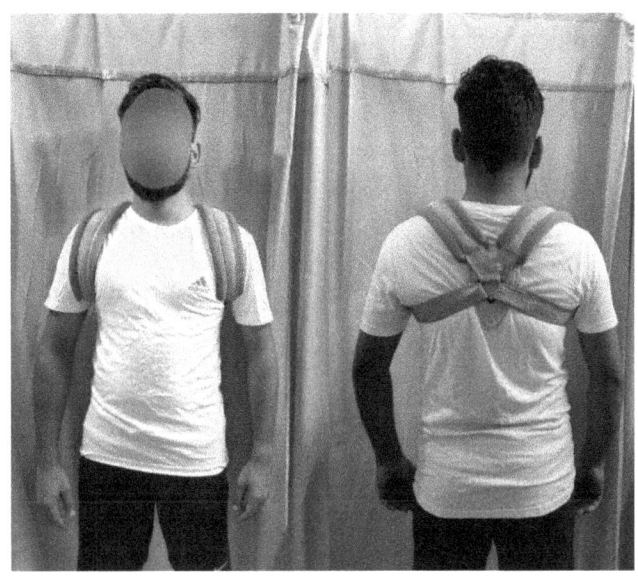

ACROMIOCLAVICULAR JOINT SUBLUXATION/DISLOCATION

Another case of a male patient aged 27 who fell onto his shoulder. This patient fell to the ground while ice skating in a mall. There is a lump over the lateral end of the clavicle. The patient can do the range of motion but it is painful. The condition is acromioclavicular subluxation.

In this condition, it's better to advice x-ray of both shoulder joint AP views for comparison.

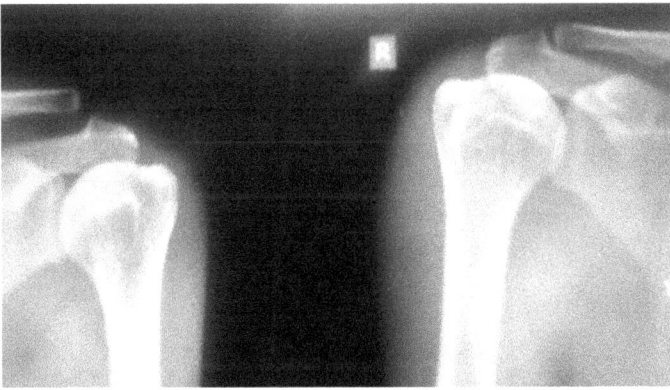

In X-ray, it's possible to visualise the subluxation of the left acromioclavicular joint. In this injury, the grade 1 injury is an acromioclavicular ligament sprain without subluxation. Grade 2 injury is acromioclavicular subluxation where the subluxation should be less than the width of the clavicle. Here conservative management shall be followed. In this condition give downward pressure to the clavicle and strapping is the better option. A sling should be advised. If the displacement is more than the width of the clavicle then it is grade 3 and must be surgically managed.

Whenever the conoid ligament and trapezoid ligament are intact then the case is subluxation or grade II acromioclavicular joint dislocation. When there is a tear in the conoid or trapezoid ligament then it is grade III dislocation. In grade III dislocation, surgical correction is needed and in grade II dislocation and subluxation, conservative management shall be done. After 3 weeks, rehabilitation to the affected shoulder is advisable.

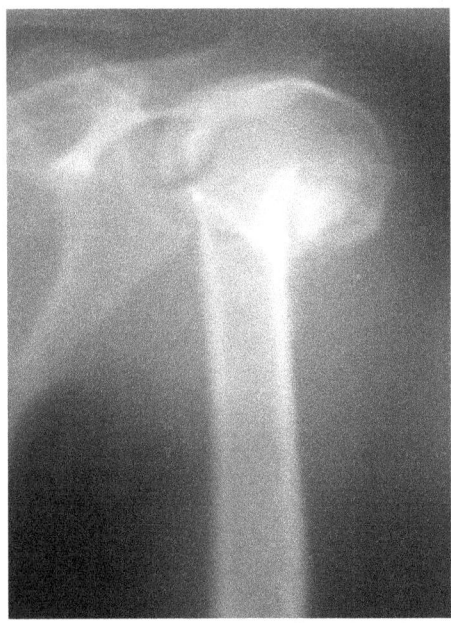

NECK OF HUMERUS FRACTURE

Another case is humerus neck fracture which is very common in old age when the patient falls on the ground hitting the shoulder. In the neck of humerus fracture especially in old age the advice given by text, Adams's Outline of Fractures is conservative management and not surgical. If there is more displacement and if the fracture is a three-part fracture, it's better to follow surgical management. But when the displacement is less and the patient is old, it's better to suggest a shoulder spica bandage for 3-4 weeks. Give early mobilization to preserve functional movements.

GREATER TUBEROSITY FRACTURE

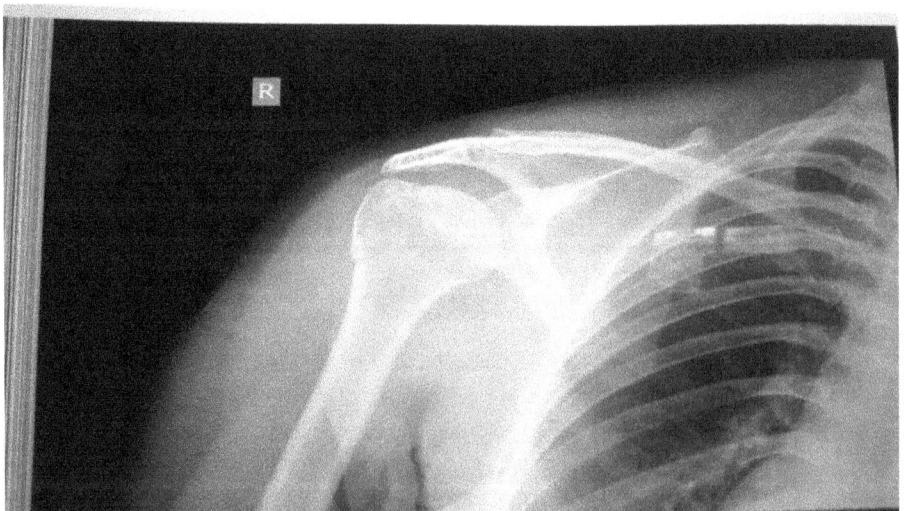

Here it's visible that the greater tuberosity fracture is without much avulsion. But most commonly greater tuberosity fracture is getting avulsed by the pull of supraspinatus muscle since it is inserted here. In the condition without avulsion, it should be managed with shoulder spica or shoulder immobilizer.

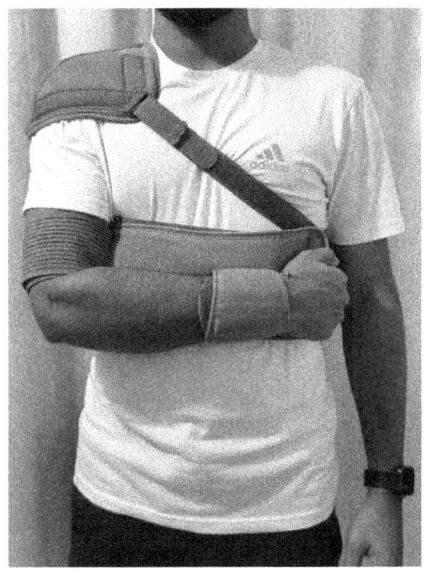

But whenever there is avulsion (all avulsion should be managed surgically except avulsion of greater tuberosity) the arm is kept in a 90° abducted position in an airplane splint.

It should be kept for 3 to 4 weeks. Then proper rehabilitation should be advised. Whenever the callus formation starts i.e., the third stage of fracture healing, the pain and tenderness reduces then the bandage shall be removed followed by rehabilitation.

BICEPS RUPTURE

Another case that is not very common is biceps injury.

A male patient aged 55 came to op with a history of sudden hold of a heavy object with sudden elbow extension. This mechanism of injury causes biceps rupture.

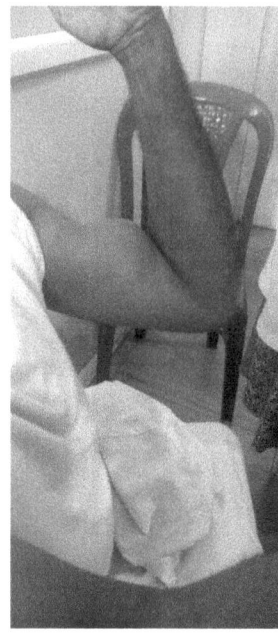
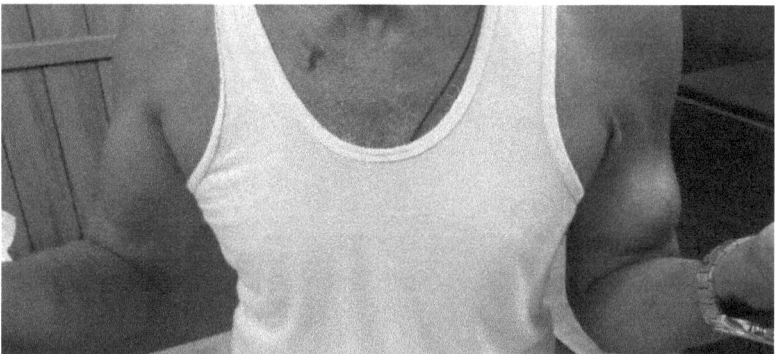

Ask the patient to flex the elbow at 90°, it's possible to see a swelling known as "popeye sign" on proximal biceps tendon rupture. There is no need for surgery in this case. In the initial phase advise rest with a sling for 2 weeks and later phase advise rehabilitation.

X-RAY SHOULDER

Regarding shoulder joint, most commonly it's better to advise AP view, axillary view, and scapular Y view. Others are true AP view, lateral view, and modified axial view.

AP VIEW

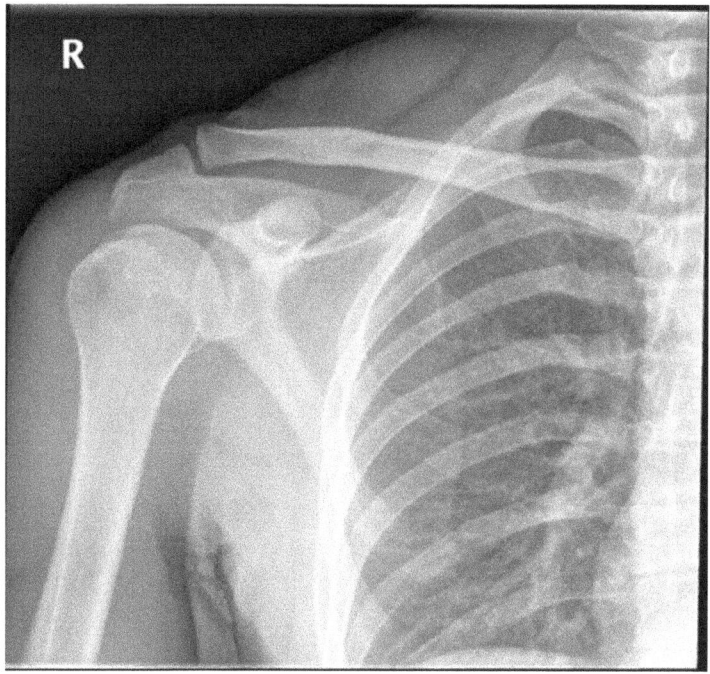

The glenohumeral joint, head of the humerus, greater tuberosity, acromion process, and acromioclavicular joint are in normal alignment.

Axillary view

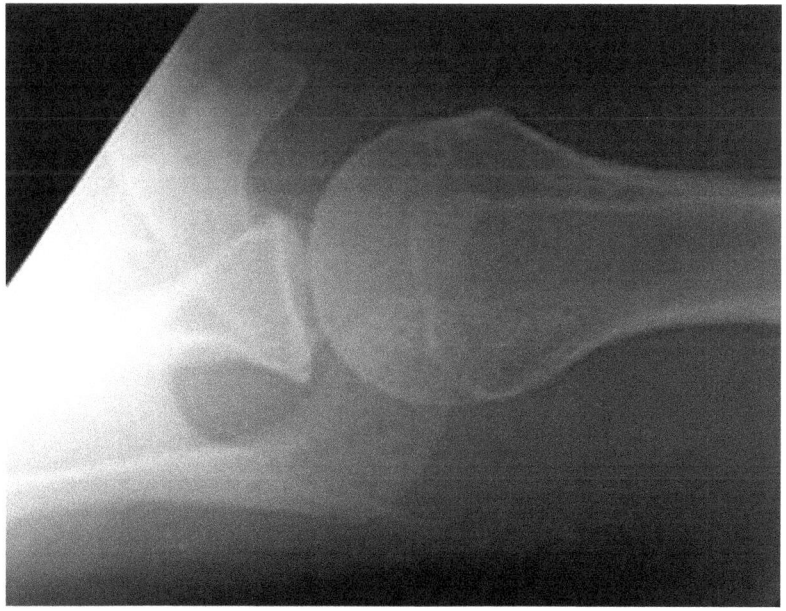

While taking an axillary view the patient should abduct his arm up to 90 degrees and if the patient can abduct his arm then only an axillary view can be advised.

Y view

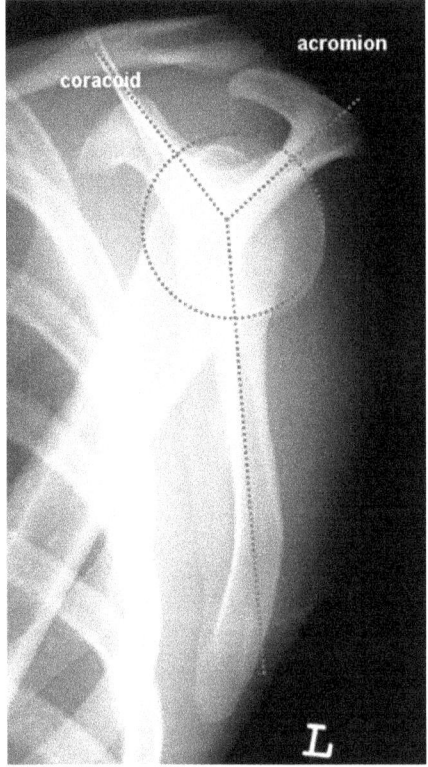

In between the coracoid process, acromion process, and the lateral border of the scapula, a Y is present. The head of the humerus is placed exactly in the middle of Y, in the normal shoulder.

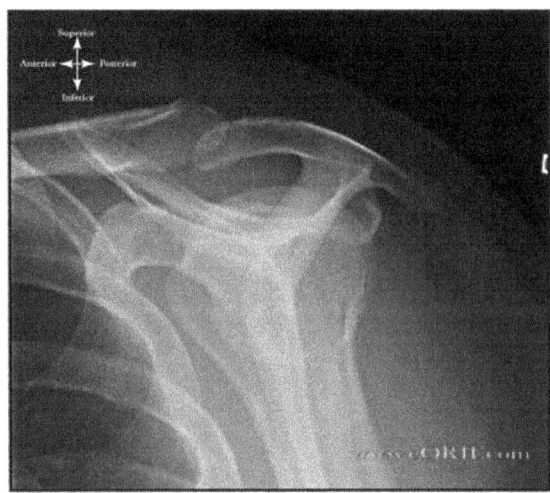

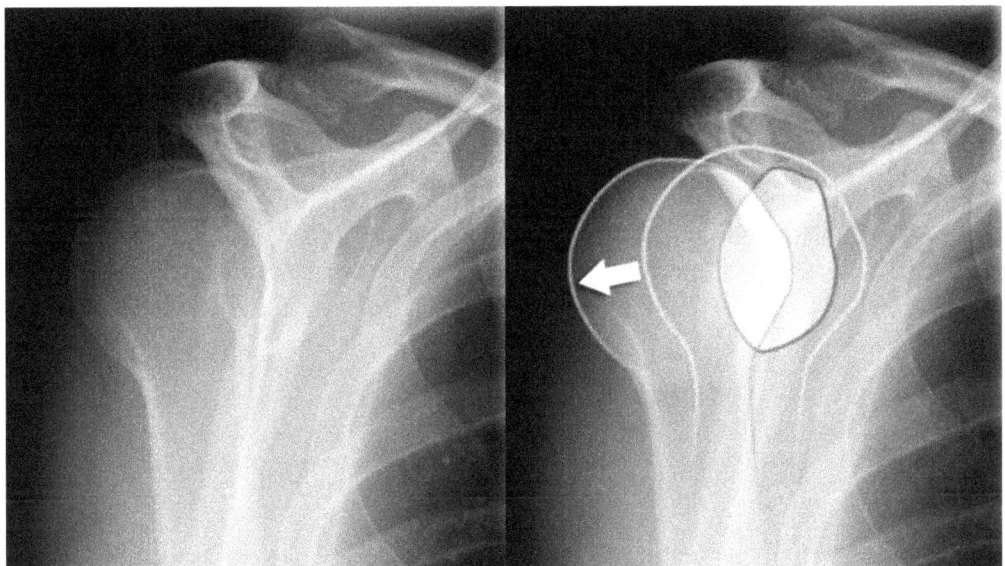

Y view helps to diagnose the displacement of the shoulder joint. Y view is more commonly advised in posterior dislocation of the shoulder joint.

DISLOCATION OF THE SHOULDER JOINT

Whenever the head of the humerus is displaced and loses contact with the glenoid cavity the condition is called dislocation of the shoulder.

The shoulder is the most common joint to dislocate as stability is compromised for mobility when compared to other joints.

Commonly seen in adults and seldom in children. Children start dislocation after teenage more commonly. One exception is pulled elbow, subluxation of the head of radius, which is common in the age group 2-5 years.

Broadly dislocation is classified into two groups, acute and recurrent.

Acute dislocation

is again classified into

1. Anterior

2. Posterior
3. Subglenoid dislocation or luxatio erecta.

The most common dislocation is anterior dislocation. It includes about 90% of dislocations of the shoulder joint.

- Anterior dislocation:- The head of the humerus lies in front of the glenoid cavity.
- Posterior dislocation:- The head of the humerus lies behind the glenoid cavity.
- Subglenoid dislocation:- The head of the humerus lies beneath the glenoid cavity.

Anterior dislocation

Mechanism

- fall on out-stretched hand
- direct force blow from the posterior aspect of the shoulder
- rarely due to falling onto the shoulder

On examination

Undress the patient up to the waist.

Inspection

- Normal contour is lost.
- Flattening of the shoulder joint.

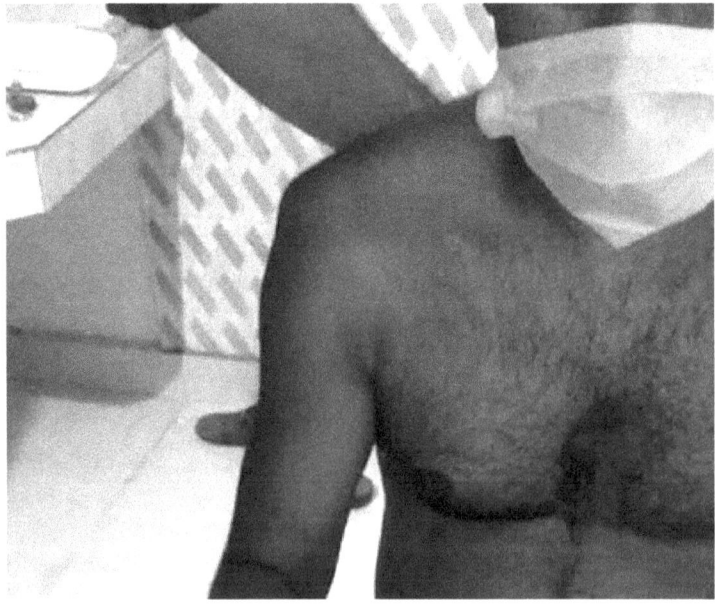

NOTE :

The flattening of deltoid muscle may also occur in a pathological condition for example glenohumeral joint arthritis, rheumatoid arthritis, or TB shoulder joint. Here the flattening occurs due to wasting of the deltoid but on palpation, it's possible to feel the greater tuberosity. So make sure of anterior dislocation with the protocol of inspection, palpation, dugas, and x-ray. Otherwise simply seeing a flattening of the shoulder, if you attempt reduction in above said conditions, it ends in a fracture of the neck of the humerus due to weakness.

Palpation

The head of the humerus is displaced anteriorly so that the head of the humerus is either subcoracoid or sub-clavicular and it's possible to feel the acromion process over the most lateral aspect.

Subcoracoid dislocation

The head of the humerus usually lies below the coracoid process in front of the neck of the scapula.

Subclavicular dislocation

The head of the humerus may lie below the clavicle in the Delto pectoral groove.

Regarding the range of motion that makes the basic clinical examination, the patient is unwilling to attempt any movements due to shoulder dislocation. Due to immense pain and due to the displacement of the head of the humerus, the patient is unwilling to do any movements.

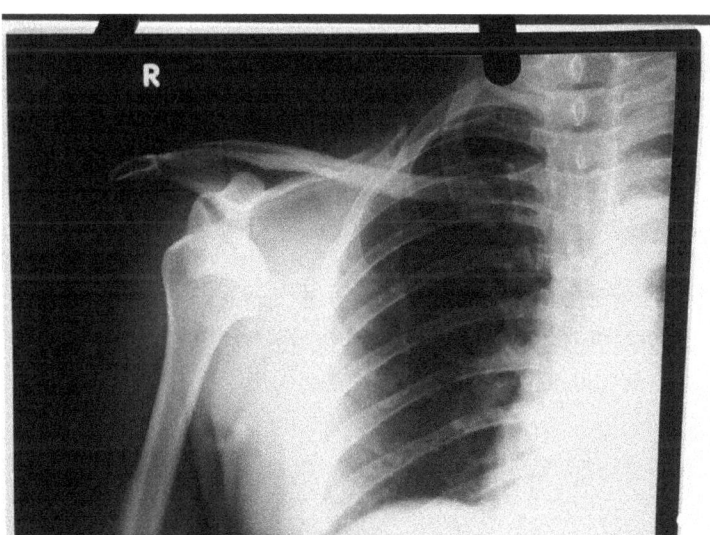

X-ray AP view of the shoulder joint shows the anterior dislocation of a shoulder joint.

Special examination mainly includes Duga's test

DUGA'S TEST

In dislocation of the shoulder, the patient is unable to touch the opposite shoulder with the hand of the affected side while the arm is kept in contact by the side of the chest. After the reduction this test helps to check if the reduction is perfect.

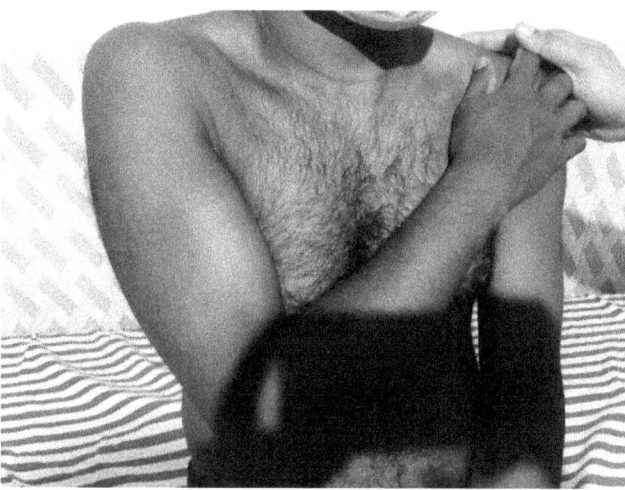

This is a normal dugas test which can only be done with a normal shoulder joint. Dugas test can't be done with an anteriorly dislocated shoulder.

NOTE:

In acute supraspinatus partial tears, the patient is unable to do the dugas test. Never attempt reduction only by checking pain and dugas. An attempt of a reduction method in supraspinatus partial tears makes it a complete tear. So always follow the basic protocol of look, feel, move, special examination, and radiological investigation before attempting reduction for the patient's benefit and to avoid medicolegal cases.

Hamilton ruler test-Normally a straight ruler cannot be made to touch acromion process and lateral epicondyle of the humerus due to the presence of Greater tuberosity of the humerus. But this becomes possible in the anterior dislocation of the shoulder.

Callaway's test -the vertical circumference of the axilla is increased in comparison to the other side.

Bryant's test-Anterior and posterior folds of the axilla are at different levels in the dislocated shoulder.

Reduction method

Hippocrates method: a stockinged toe is kept inside the affected axilla and traction to the affected upper limb is applied. This is explained by Acharya Sushruta

" मुसलेनोत्क्षिपेत् कक्षामंससन्धौ विसंहते ॥

स्थानस्थितं च बध्नीयात् स्वस्तिकेन विचक्षणः ॥ " (SU.CHI 3)

Kocher's method

The most popular method. It includes

- **T**raction along the line of the humerus
- **E**xternal rotation of the arm
- **A**dduction up to the midline of the chest
- **M**edial rotation of the arm

Also known as **TEAM**

There is a chance of injury to the axillary nerve in this condition leading to loss of sensation of the deltoid muscle known as regimental badge sign. This condition is a neuropraxia and can be reversed within a span of 2 weeks to 4 weeks.

NB. Nerve injury classification by Seddon-

1. Neuropraxia-mild
2. Axonotmesis -moderate
3. Neurotmesis- severe and bad prognosis

3 weeks of immobilization is a must for anterior shoulder dislocation and every dislocation for the healing of the joint capsule. After 3 weeks rehabilitation is very important to avoid recurrent dislocations.

Posterior dislocation of shoulder joint

It is rare when compared to anterior dislocation.

Mechanism

- -by direct blow on the front of the shoulder.
- -Forced internal rotation of the abducted arm.

Most commonly there will be a history of epileptiform convulsion or an electric shock in which the patient is not able to fall on the outstretched arm. When there is a fall on the outstretched hand most commonly anterior dislocation will occur but here the direct hit on the front may cause a posterior dislocation of the shoulder joint which may be bilateral. So check the other joint to rule out whether it's bilateral.

Attitude

This differentiates the condition.

The attitude is an internally rotated arm and the patient is not able to externally rotate the arm even up to normal. This is the most important diagnostic feature of posterior dislocation of the shoulder.

The second thing, in the anterior aspect of the acromion process, there is flattening. The third point is, the Acromion process and coracoid process will be more prominent in posterior dislocation. Coming to normal AP view x-ray there is a chance of misdiagnosis of this condition. We may overlook this condition because the only difference is the medial rotation of the head of the humerus. This particular condition is known as daylight sign or walking stick sign in X-ray AP view of posterior dislocation of shoulder.

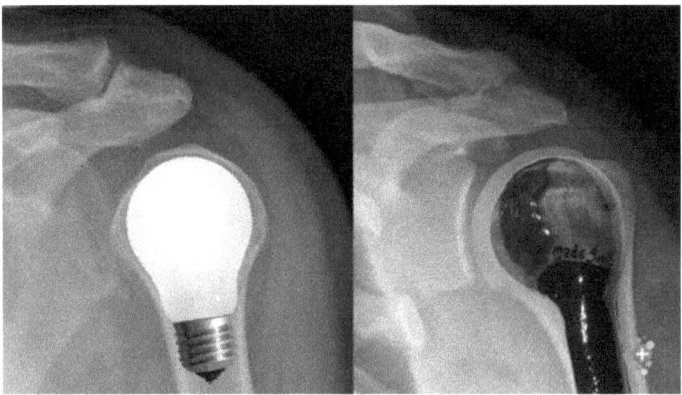

The axillary view or axial view helps to diagnose posterior dislocation. But it is very difficult because the patient should abduct his arm up to 90 degrees for this view which is very difficult in a dislocated arm.

The suitable view to identify posterior dislocation is the Y view or trans scapular view.

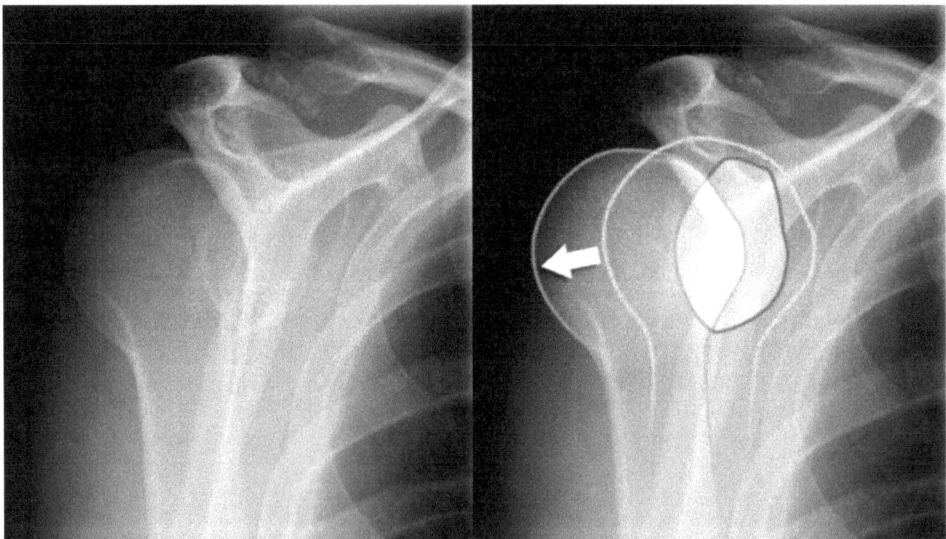

In the posterior dislocation of the shoulder joint, the head of the humerus is displaced posteriorly and is not at the center of **Y**. So if a patient comes to the OPD with a history of epileptiform convulsion or electric shock and the patient is not able to attempt any movements and second thing in attitude, the patient's arm is internally rotated and not possible to externally rotate arm even up to normal, prefer Y view to diagnose posterior dislocation.

Reduction of posterior dislocation of the shoulder

Traction

External rotation and

Abduction simultaneously

It shall be learned as **TEA** (Here A is abduction and in TEAM for anterior shoulder dislocation, A is adduction)

Subglenoid Dislocation of the shoulder joint

Rare type of shoulder dislocation where the arm is held in abduction.

The head of the humerus is placed beneath the glenoid cavity.

Attitude of the patient is unable to do the adduction of the affected arm and is kept always in an abducted position with the help of another arm. X-ray shoulder AP view is needed for the diagnosis.

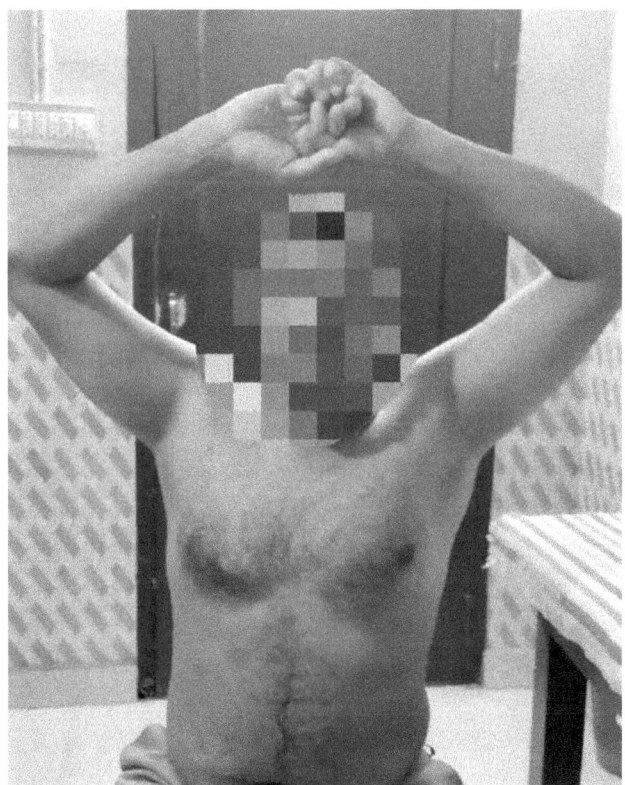

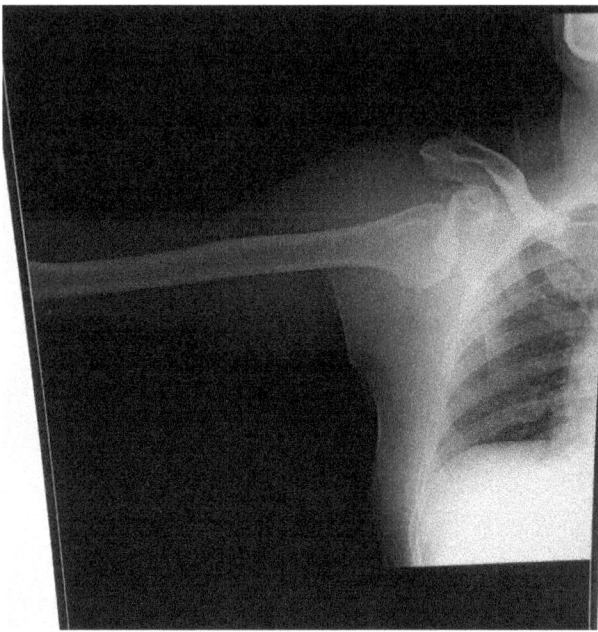 inferior dislocation

The reduction method is traction along with proper counter traction.

Reduction is usually obtained by applying traction in abduction and swinging the arm into the adduction position. With another hand, the surgeon should push the head of the humerus up into the glenoid cavity. Immobilisation is done using a shoulder spica or shoulder immobilizer.

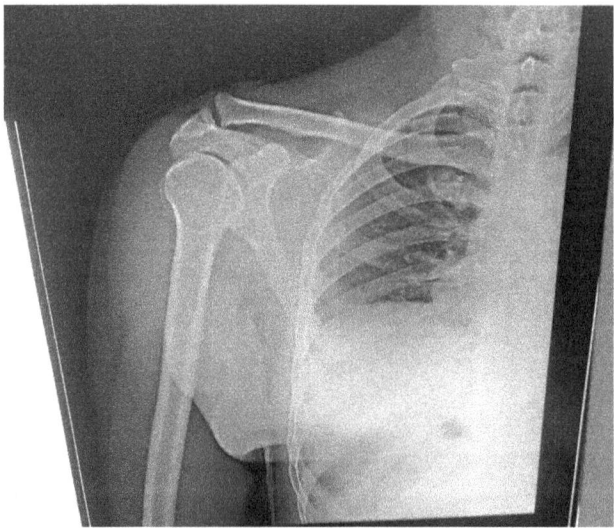 after reduction

This condition is very rare but it may happen to people traveling in a vehicle when the vehicle suddenly applies brakes and their arm is in the abducted position like holding the handlebar at the roof of the bus. Here due to inertia, the patient's body will move forward but the arms stay in the position. This injury may also occur in RTA, rarely.

Recurrent dislocation of the shoulder joint

The reason for recurrent dislocation of the shoulder joint is the tear in the shoulder capsule and detachment of the glenoid labrum. It is very important in acute dislocation of the shoulder joint to keep the arm in 3 weeks of immobilization either with a shoulder spica bandage or with shoulder immobilizer and then after immobilization ask the patient to do rehabilitation properly to avoid recurrent dislocation. Whenever a patient comes to OPD with dislocation whether it is acute or recurrent we aim to manage that particular dislocation. It should be reduced within a short time and then a shoulder X-ray should be taken to confirm reduction and 3 weeks immobilization should be given. After 3 weeks of immobilization rehabilitation should be done. When the patient comes to OPD and says that the patient has recurrent dislocation, then definitely it's a must to check the apprehension test.

Apprehension test.

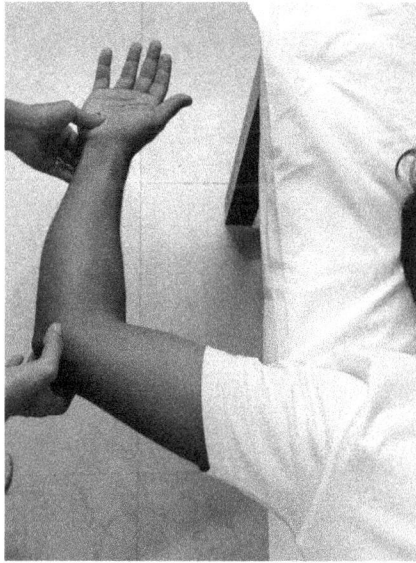

If the patient's arm is placed passively behind the coronal plane in a position of abduction and external rotation, the patient immediately resists and apprehends.

If needed it's better to advice an MRI to rule out Bankart and Hill-Sachs lesions in recurrent shoulder dislocation.

In Recurrent shoulder dislocation, the anterior rim of the glenoid cavity is affected; this is called Bankart lesion. The posterolateral aspect of the head of the humerus affected is known as the Hills Sachs lesion. Both will definitely occur in recurrent dislocation of the shoulder.

Regarding the surgical operation, the putti-platt and Bankart's operation are options.

In putti Platt operation, which is not common nowadays, double breastment of the subscapularis muscle is done to prevent the external rotation of the affected arm. In bankart's operation, the anterior rent of the glenoid capsule is corrected.

AYURVEDIC MANAGEMENT OF RECURRENT SHOULDER DISLOCATION

The primary aim is to avoid recurrent shoulder dislocation. So the patient should refrain from activities leading to recurrence, such as simultaneous abduction and external rotation, as nidana parivarjana.

To strengthen the affected area mainly rotator cuff muscles, ligaments attached to that area, pectoral area muscles, and the muscles attached to the thoracoscapular region, it's advisable to adopt :

1. Nasya with gandha taila

2. Pichu with brimhana taila

3. Brumhana Upanaha to strengthen muscles of shoulder

4. Sekam or Dhara with ksheera, brimhana taila

5. Sarasa or mamsarasa annalepanam.

6. Exercise: Rehabilitation is the most important thing for recurrent shoulder dislocation. Active use and exercise, active use and exercise against resistance and active use and exercise with weight-bearing are the three phases of rehab. Each phase should be given in a gap and ask the patient to continue it for a while.

7. Internal use and nasya of Dhanwantara/ ksheerabala avarthi.

8. Internal medication: Gandha taila and Laksha guggulu.

9. Matravasthi with danwanthara taila

प्रशाखास्वनुवासनम् (SU.CHI 3) is explained as bhagnanathara kriya

This protocol is found to be effective in recurrent shoulder dislocation.

CLINICAL EXAMINATION FOR SUPERIOR LABRAL TEAR ANTERIOR TO POSTERIOR (SLAP) TEAR

Slap tears may occur due to repeated overhead activities. Whenever there is a slap tear the orthopedician suggested surgical reconstruction earlier. But nowadays isolated injury to the labrum is not surgically managed because the functional outcome is not very good. Before taking an MRI one should do the clinical examination.

It's recommended to follow the clinical examination, biceps load 2 test and speed test.

<u>Biceps load 2</u>

The biceps load 2 test is a clinical examination maneuver used to assess for a SLAP (Superior Labral tear Anterior to Posterior) tear in the shoulder joint. The test involves the following steps:

Positioning: The patient's arm is abducted to 120°.

Apprehension: In this position, the patient may feel apprehension, as if the shoulder joint is about to dislocate.

Supination: The examiner performs the supination of the patient's forearm.

Relief of Apprehension: Supination often relieves the patient's apprehension.

Resistance: The patient is then asked to flex the elbow against resistance in the 120° abduction position.

Pain Assessment: Pain is assessed, and the presence of pain over the anterior capsule during this maneuver can be indicative of a SLAP tear, specifically from 12 o'clock to 3 o'clock.

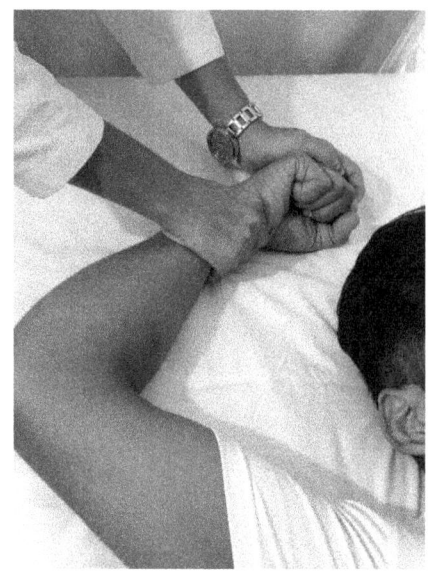

Palpation

Palpation of the anterior capsule in the shoulder can be a valuable component of a clinical examination to assess labral tears. The anterior capsule is an important anatomical region, and tenderness or discomfort during palpation may indicate potential issues with the labrum. To perform this examination:

Identify Landmarks:

- Locate the point of attachment of the supraspinatus tendon on the anterolateral aspect.
- Identify the attachment of the subscapularis tendon just below anteriorly.
- Locate the coracoid process anteriorly.
- Visualize the triangle formed by connecting these three points.

    Palpate the Anterior Capsule:

- Palpate the area in the middle of the triangle, which represents the anterior capsule.
- Assess the tenderness on palpation.

Tenderness in the region of the anterior capsule could suggest issues such as a labral tear or other anterior shoulder pathology. However, it's important to consider other clinical findings and use this information as part of a comprehensive evaluation for a more accurate diagnosis. Additionally, imaging studies may be required for a definitive diagnosis of labral tears.

Speed test

Ask the patient to elevate his arm against our resistance. It will be positive in labral pathologies. It's also a test for biceps tendonitis.

Please note that minimum clinical examinations should be done on a single patient. All these tests are provocative tests and the patient will feel pain doing all these maneuvers.

NB. SLAP tear recent research studies[1]

The management of SLAP (Superior Labrum Anterior to Posterior) lesions involves a comprehensive approach tailored to the specific characteristics and symptoms of the individual. The management strategies can be categorized into four broad groups:

1. Nonoperative Management:

- This approach involves conservative measures and exercises.
- Scapular exercises are emphasized, along with efforts to restore balanced musculature.
- Typically, this nonoperative management is expected to provide relief for about two-thirds of patients.

2. SLAP Repair:

- Patients with a clear traumatic episode and symptoms of instability may benefit from SLAP repair.
- For patients younger than 40, SLAP repair without biceps tenotomy or tenodesis may be considered.
- For patients aged 40 and older, combining SLAP repair with biceps tenotomy or tenodesis might be recommended.

3. Biceps Tenotomy or Tenodesis:

- Patients with overuse etiology and without symptoms of instability may be managed with biceps tenotomy or tenodesis.
- This approach is particularly suitable for those where surgical intervention is indicated but SLAP repair is not deemed necessary.

4. Rigorous Physical Therapy for Throwing Athletes:

- Throwing athletes should undergo rigorous physical therapy.

- Emphasis should be on hip, core, and scapular exercises, in addition to restoring shoulder motion and achieving a balanced rotator cuff.

APABAHUKA POSSIBILITIES

1. Cervical radiculopathy
2. Clavicle fracture
3. Shoulder dislocation
4. Fracture neck of the humerus
5. Supraspinatus tear
6. Brachial plexus injury
7. Erb's paralysis
8. Greater tuberosity fracture
9. Diabetic brachial plexopathy

It's possible to add some other pathologies that will affect shoulder abduction. So diagnosis with clinical examination and relevant investigations is a must. It helps us in the assessment of prognosis, determining how much relief in how many days, making prescriptions precise, providing specific management, and deciding whether a bandage is indicated or not, needs outpatient or inpatient treatment, and for how many days inpatient treatment is needed. It will provide clarity and sharpness, in our management, and in the explanation of prognosis to the patient. Maintaining ethical standards necessitates an adherence to scientific methodology. Our aim should always be Sudha Chikitsa (avoid recurrence), cost-effectiveness, and maintaining scientific temperament (with our technical terminology, it must be possible in explaining the logic of the result in each condition to a BAMS graduate).

Pathya of shoulder

- Proper talakkenna
- Proper warm up and **cool down** (before and after sports activities)
- Proper hydration with solute replacement (in sports patients to avoid recurrence)
- Correct posture while doing activities

- Avoid weight bearing in affected limb
- Avoid ratri snana
- Avoid keeping hand in place of pillow

SHOULDER REHABILITATION

The role of rehabilitation in musculoskeletal disease is crucial.

In injury, after the removal of the bandage, and in pathology from the stage after ama pachana, rehabilitation shall be advised.

Coming to the principles of rehabilitation, it includes active use and exercise in the first phase. In the second phase, exercises are performed against resistance, and in the third phase, active use and exercise with weight-bearing. This principle is mentioned in Susrutha Samhita Chikitsa Sthana in the management of hasta tala bhagna. In hasta tala bhagna, it is said,

"मृत्पिण्डं धारयेत् पूर्वं लवणं च ततः परम् ॥

हस्ते जातबले चापि कुर्यात् पाषाणधारणम् ॥" (SU.CHI 3)

It's recommended to advise rehabilitation to every patient to avoid recurrence, ensure the quality of life, and allow them to continue the activities they were doing before the injury or pathology.

Rehabilitation is very significant in the management of orthopedic or musculoskeletal conditions. In injury, immediately after the removal of the bandage, rehabilitation should be given. For example, if the shoulder is immobilized, ask the patient to move the fingers and wrist. In cases like supraspinatus tear, if the shoulder was immobilized with a shoulder immobilizer, after 2 weeks, remove the handcuff and facilitate elbow movements without mobilizing the shoulder joint. On the removal of the shoulder immobilizer after 3 weeks, shoulder rehab must be started.

Rehabilitation should be started in very small quantities and very small numbers, gradually increasing over time. The patient should not feel pain while doing or after rehabilitation.

In supraspinatus injury, after immobilization for 3 weeks, it's advisable to do rehabilitation for 6 weeks, and then it shall be stopped. However, in other conditions, such as when a patient comes to OPD with recurrent shoulder dislocation, advise the patient to continue rehabilitation continuously and regularly.

Customization is needed in rehabilitation, as it varies from patient to patient and is based on the specific condition of the patient.

The rehabilitation of the shoulder should be started with pendulum exercise.

The lumbar spine should be in flexion, the patient should stand in a stooped position and a pendulum exercise should be done. It should be done forward-backward, towards both medial and lateral sides and rotation in clockwise and anti-clockwise directions.

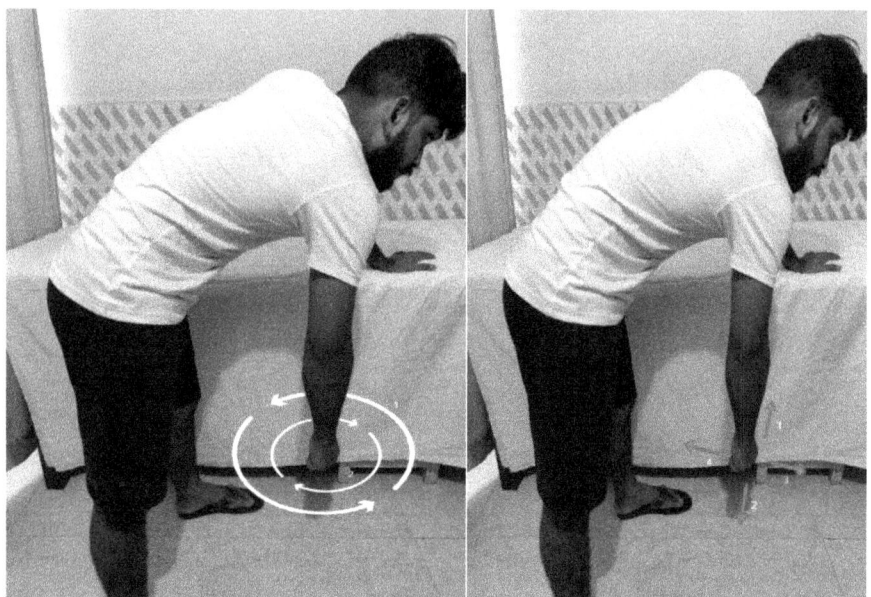

In the second phase assisted movements should be advised. Abduction with the support of the other hand shall be started. It's advisable to do pulley exercise. With the help of the normal joint, it's easily possible to do the abduction. This is very effective in almost all conditions of the shoulder joint.

Along with pulley exercise, the patient should be advised to do abduction with the support of a wall.

It can also be done by holding a stick in hand and with the help of the normal joint ask the patient to do the abduction, internal rotation, external rotation, and extension. All these movements should be done assisted or with the help of the other joint. This rehab is known as wand exercise.

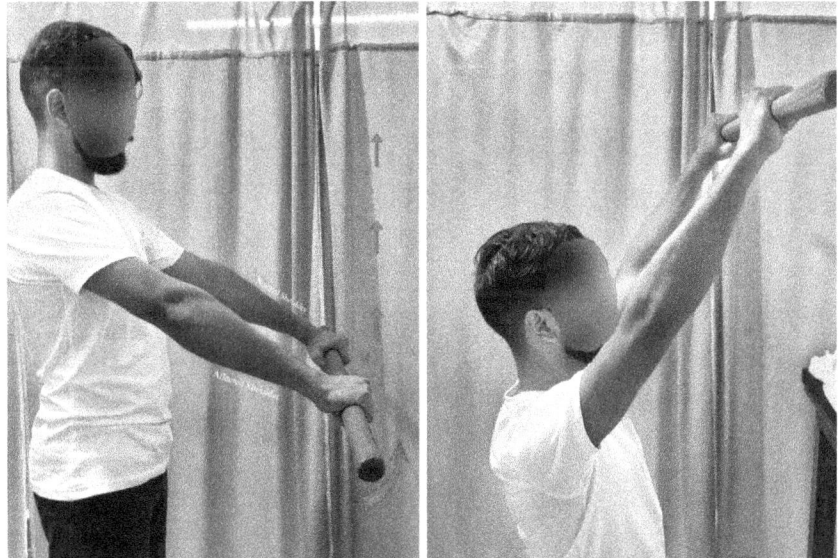

The movements of the scapula are elevation, depression, shrugging, and rotation. All these movements include movements of the scapulothoracic joint and the scapula. This is also effective in shoulder mobilization.

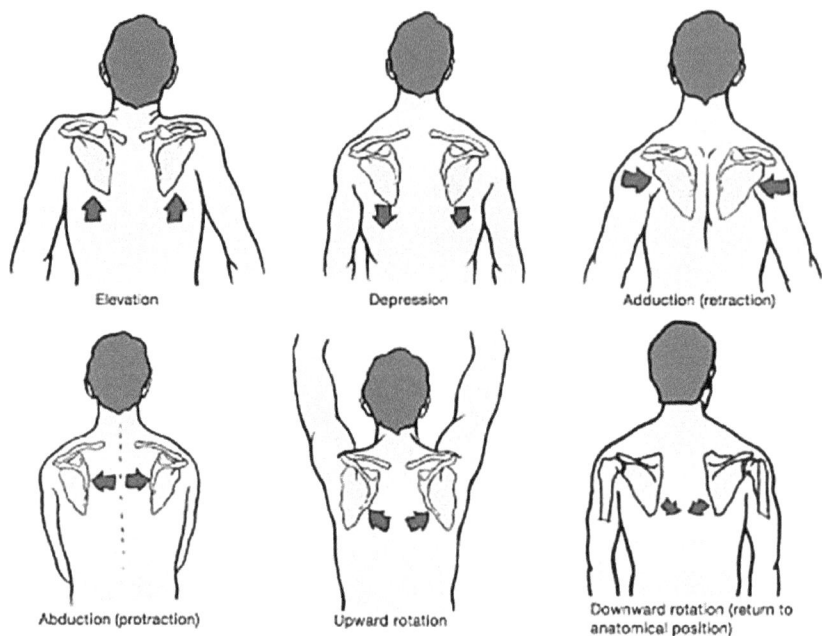

Internal rotation with support is also known as towel stretch. In peri arthritis, this exercise is very important because the patient is doing an internal rotation with the help of the normal shoulder joint which helps the patient to attain normal range.

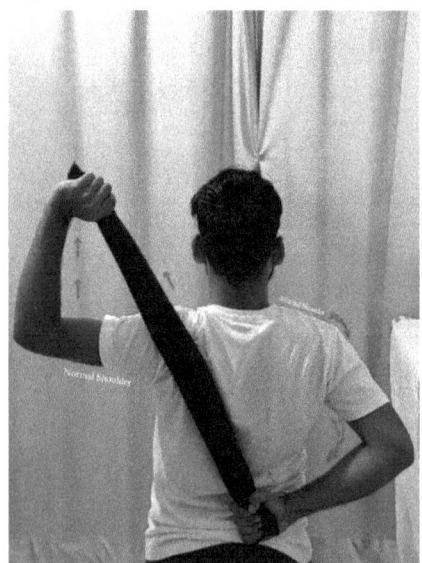

In the next phase, focus on internal rotation and external rotation against resistance using a resistance band or theraband. This should be done with a 90° flexed elbow, keeping the arm close to the body.

Following that, progress to elbow flexion and extension exercises, targeting the biceps and triceps. Begin with a 1 kg weight, followed by 2 kg and then 3 kg weights.

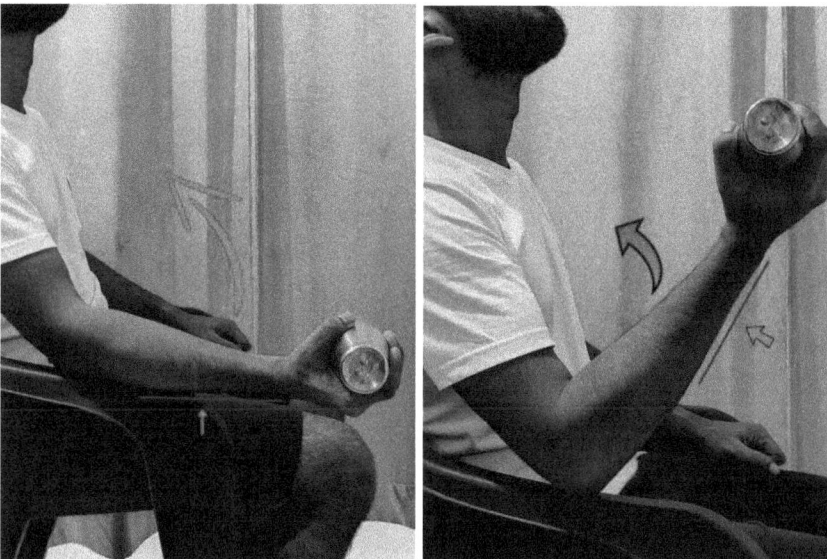

For biceps

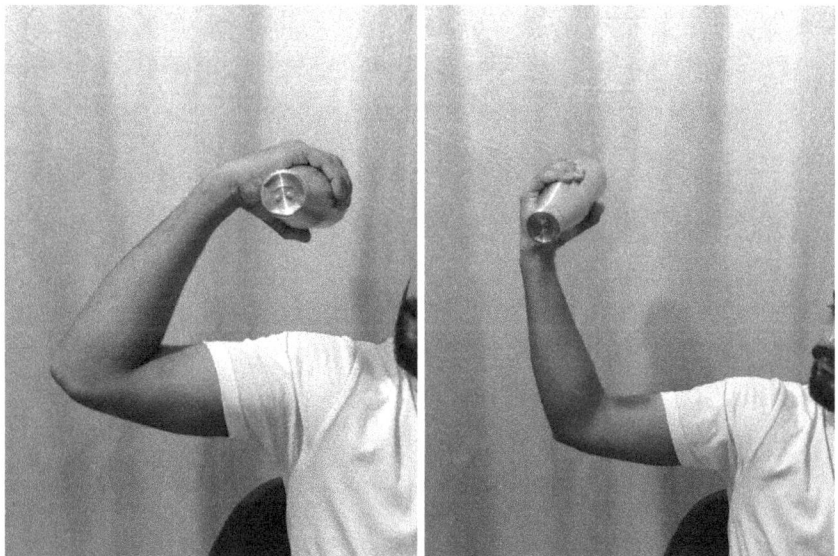

For triceps

In the last phase, instruct the patient to perform internal rotation and external rotation in a 90° abducted position with weight bearing. Gradually increase the weight, starting from 1 kg, then progressing to 2 kg, and finally 3 kg.

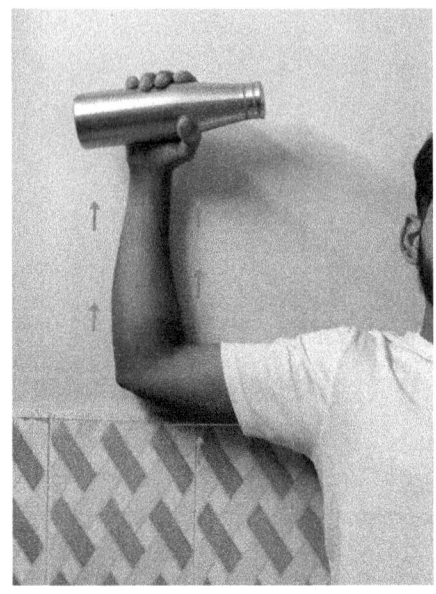

external rotation in ninety degree abduction

internal rotation in ninety degree abduction

Questions for self practice

1. Empty can test is a test for the diagnosis of which muscle
2. Reasons for painful arc syndrome
3. Clinical examination test for anterior shoulder dislocation
4. Clinical examination test for biceps tendonitis
5. Apprehension test is for the diagnosis of
6. Management of clavicle fracture

Shoulder phase 1 rehabilitation

Shoulder phase 2 rehabilitation

Shoulder phase 3 rehabilitation

CASE PRESENTATION
ANTERIOR SHOULDER DISLOCATION -MILCH METHOD OF REDUCTION

Injury

The patient was playing volleyball and at the time of the smash the patient felt severe pain over his shoulder. The patient is unable to move the affected shoulder joint and the condition is very much painful.

Here the provisional diagnosis includes anterior dislocation of the shoulder joint. It is the most common dislocation in the shoulder joint. In anterior dislocation the attitude will be patient, supporting the affected hand with the opposite hand.

In every examination of shoulder joints, undress the patient up to the waist to compare both joints. On inspection, flattening of the shoulder joint is visible.

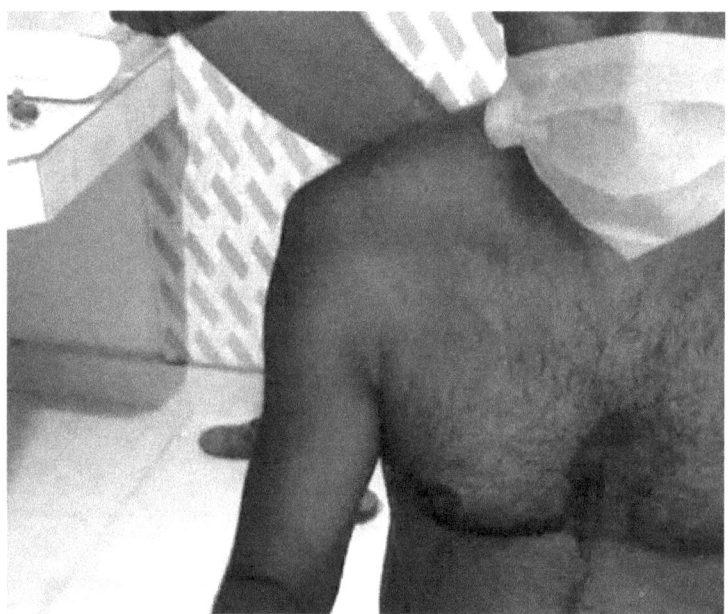

Normal contour is lost and squared-off appearance is there because the head of the humerus is displaced anteriorly and inferiorly. It is displaced from the glenoid cavity. It's possible to visualize the acromion process most laterally.

Clinical examination

The clinical examination is the Dugas test

Ask the patient to touch the opposite shoulder along the line of the chest and the patient is not able to do this test. The patient is unable to attempt any movement. On palpation, it's possible to palpate the acromion process on the most lateral aspect and the head of the humerus below the coracoid process.

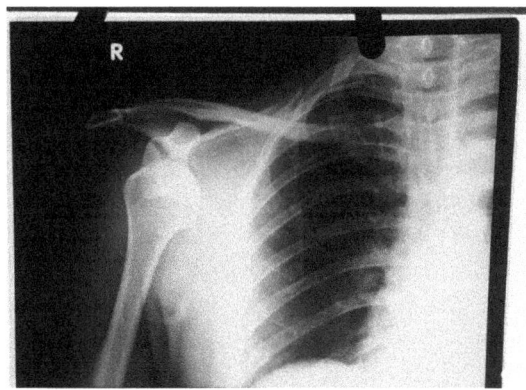

X-ray AP view Anterior shoulder dislocation.

The reduction method adopted is Milch or modified Kocher's method (very easy method of reduction).

Patient is advised to lie in supine position.

- Raise the affected shoulder to simultaneous external rotation and abduction posture, which is not painful.
- **Traction along the line of the humerus** (reduction happens at once with traction itself in recurrent anterior shoulder dislocations)
- **External rotation** (reduction occurs in fresh cases at this stage)
- By doing these two methods itself in abduction and external rotation gives reduction of anterior shoulder dislocation.
- Adduction and Medial rotation is done together by placing the thumb in the axilla.

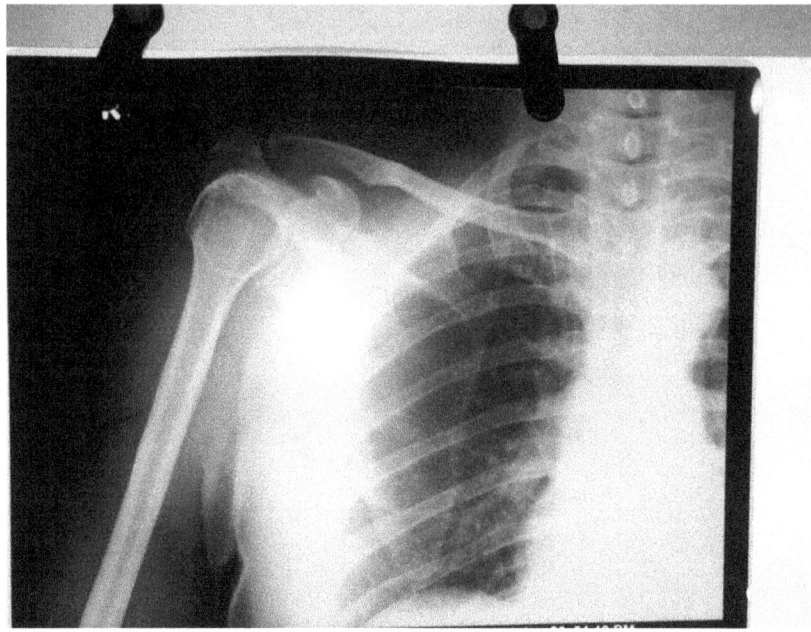 after reduction

In the adducted position the shoulder is immobilized using a shoulder immobilizer

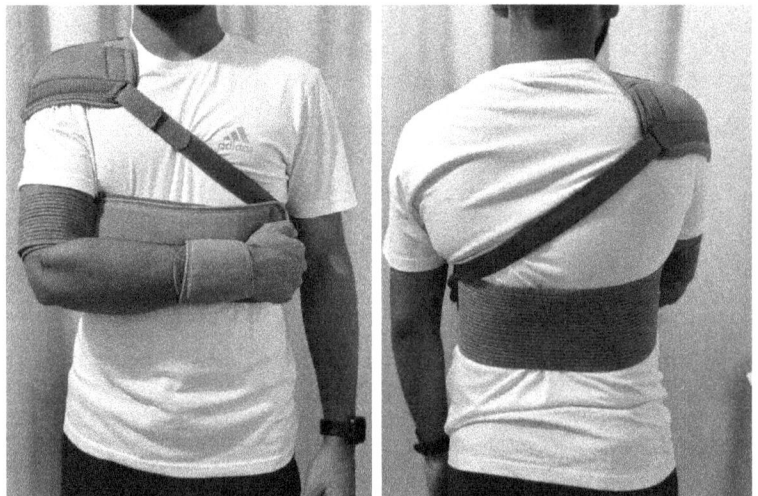

and kept for 3 weeks. Sling is not needed, if shoulder immobilizer is advised.

In any dislocation, the recommended period of immobilization is 3 weeks. This duration allows for the healing of the joint capsule tear, soft tissue injury, and the torn glenoid labrum. If a shoulder spica bandage is applied, a sling shall also be advised. After the initial 3 weeks, proper rehabilitation should be initiated to prevent further recurrence. It's crucial to note that if the patient is not immobilized for the full 3 weeks, there is an increased risk of recurrent dislocation.

Regimental badge sign is a complication that can occur in shoulder joint dislocation. This complication involves a loss of sensation due to axillary nerve injury during the reduction of the shoulder joint dislocation. The loss of sensation is specifically over the deltoid muscle where the badge of army officers are typically worn. This condition is reversible and tends to improve within 2 to 4 weeks, as it's a neuropraxia.

The Milch method of reduction is considered a gentle technique for reducing shoulder joint dislocations. This approach aims to minimize complications such as the regimental badge sign, which involves axillary nerve injury during the reduction process. By employing the Milch method, healthcare providers aim to reduce the risk of adverse effects and ensure a smoother and less traumatic reduction of the shoulder joint.

SUMMARY OF SHOULDER INJURY AND PATHOLOGY

It is crucial to evaluate the cervical spine in cases of shoulder joint pain. The most common cause of shoulder joint pain is cervical radiculopathy, typically from C4-C5 and C5-C6, causing pain over the shoulder radiating up to the mid-arm or elbow.

When a patient presents with shoulder joint pain, the initial assessment should include Apley's scratch test. This involves checking for internal rotation, where the patient attempts to touch the opposite scapula's medial border, and external rotation and abduction simultaneously. If these tests are possible without pain or restriction, it is essential to conduct a cervical spine examination, including the Spurling and cervical flexion rotation tests, to rule out cervical disc disease.

Management of injury

Immediately after an injury, as part of first aid, the use of a sling is recommended. Rest is considered a primary aspect of initial care.

Sheetha prayoga is advised in Susrutha Samhita during the initial phase of bhagna. The rationale is that, after an injury, hematoma formation occurs due to fractures, muscle strains, or ligament sprains. To reduce hematoma formation and mitigate complications, Sheetha prayoga is recommended. Murivenna, with half of its ingredients having a sheeta effect, the other half being Teekshna, and with a sheetha base Kera, is suggested. This aids in reducing swelling and soft tissue injuries in the affected area. It's important to note that Murivenna should not be applied as abhyanga (massage) but should be poured at the time of bandaging, and patients are instructed to pour Murivenna on the affected side.

NB. Murivenna is a wonder drug for burns and scalds too.

It's advisable to put a bandage on immediatelyto reduce the pain and swelling .

Management of pathology

Here pathology means peri arthritis, supraspinatus tendonitis, biceps tendonitis, and acromioclavicular joint osteoarthritis. In these conditions primary management includes

Amasophahara: in all pathologies, there is inflammation associated with morning stiffness. So the initial phase includes ama sopha hara.

Special procedures including raktamoksha, srungam, and agnikarma shall be advisable, as per the condition.

Internal Sneha must be started after ama sopha hara management.

Rasayana selection is always based on dhatu.

Yoga and rehabilitation are incorporated as per the condition. In pathological conditions after ama pachana rehabilitation is advisable. When the patient starts rehabilitation without ama pachana, there is a chance of aggravation of symptoms. All the movements of the shoulder joint is advisable in the initial phase. All the movements against resistance are advised in the second phase. In the third phase all the movements with weight bearing are recommended.

Nutritional support is very important in musculoskeletal conditions with degeneration. All pathological conditions require proper care and nutrition. "What your doctor doesn't know about nutritional medicine may be killing you" written by Ray D Strand, shall be read to know more about nutritional aspects.

TO AVOID RECURRENCE

To prevent recurrence in injuries and promote overall well-being, rehabilitation, Rasayana, and internal snehapana are essential tools to be followed.

For sports injuries, emphasizing proper warm-up and cool-down routines before and after activities is crucial.

Additionally, maintaining proper hydration is important, and solute replacement therapy should be considered to avoid overhydration without sufficient solutes. Referring to classical Ayurvedic texts like Susrutha Samhita (Chikitsa Sthana, Su. Chi. 2 & 3), fluid replacement recommendations include adding saindhava with mamsa rasa, peya, and vilepi. Proper hydration with solute replacement is especially important for athletes to support their continued activities.

Nutritional support plays a vital role in achieving better results and preventing recurrence. Adequate intake of essential nutrients supports overall health and recovery. A balanced diet with natural sources of fruits and vegetables are found to be effective.

Incorporating yoga and pranayama into the routine can be effective for managing sports injuries and psychosomatic diseases, contributing to both physical and mental well-being.

Quick examination and nutshell of management

Shrugging at the time of abduction is due to supraspinatus tendonitis or supraspinatus tendon tear.

Pain in the mid range of abduction and absence of pain in the extremities is suggestive of painful arc syndrome. It is due to 5 causes which are supraspinatus tendonitis, supraspinatus tendon tear, calcification of supraspinatus muscle, greater tuberosity fracture, and subacromial bursitis.

Sharp pain felt only above 150° of abduction is due to ac joint arthritis.

The whole range of abduction is painful in glenohumeral joint arthritis which is not much common when compared to ac joint arthritis.

Abduction and medial rotation are restricted in Adhesive capsulitis. It includes 3 stages, the first stage is increasing pain. The second stage is decreasing pain and increasing stiffness and in 3rd stage, decreasing stiffness

Empty can test is done for supraspinatus tendonitis and Supraspinatus partial tear.

Drop arm test is positive in the complete tear of supraspinatus.

Apley's Scratch test serves as a fundamental clinical examination for evaluating shoulder joint pathology in the early stages. It provides a quick assessment of the shoulder joint's normalcy or any underlying issues when a patient presents with shoulder pain in the OPD.

Kocher's method of reduction is employed in cases of anterior shoulder dislocation. The process involves traction along the humerus line, counter traction, external rotation in the subsequent phase, and, in the final stage, adduction up to the midline of the chest while maintaining external rotation and concluding with medial rotation.

Milch method includes only traction and external rotation in the abducted and externally rotated shoulder.

CLINICAL PEARLS SHOULDER

Shrugging at time of abduction
- Supraspinatus tendonitis

Pain in midrange of abduction and extremes painless
- Painful arc syndrome

Sharp pain felt only above 150° of abduction
- AC joint arthritis

Whole range of abduction painful
- Arthritis of glenohumeral joint

Medial rotation, external rotation and abduction restricted
- Adhesive capsulitis

Pain is the feature in
- Tendinopathy
- Impingement
- sprain/strain
- labral pathology

Mechanical block is seen in
- labral pathology
- frozen shoulder

Night pain (lying on affected shoulder) is typically seen in
- rotator cuff pathology
- anterior shoulder instability
- ACJ injury
- neoplasm (particularly unremitting)

Sensation of 'clicking or clunking are the features seen in
- labral pathology
- unstable shoulder (either anterior or multidirectional instability)

Sensation of stiffness or instability is the feature of
- frozen shoulder
- anterior or multidirectional instability

NB. It's important to note that **primary parkinsonism,** where the upper limb is affected unilaterally, can manifest as unilateral shoulder pain. Upon examination, a diagnosis of adhesive capsulitis may be determined. This presentation is linked to bradykinesia, and the primary focus should be on managing the underlying Parkinson's disease.

5. ELBOW JOINT

The elbow is the most notorious joint due to complications. It easily becomes stiff.

Applied Anatomy

The Humeroulnar joint functions as a hinge joint, representing the true elbow joint responsible for facilitating flexion and extension. In contrast, the superior radioulnar joint operates as a pivot joint, enabling supination and pronation movements.

Four prominent bony points contribute to the structure: the olecranon process, medial epicondyle, lateral epicondyle, and head of the radius.

The carrying angle, the normal outward deviation of supinated and extended forearm with respect to arm, is a noteworthy feature (11° to 13° in males and 13° to 15° in females). This angle aids in clearing the pelvis during arm swings in walking, a process essential for reducing air resistance and maintaining balance.

The stability of the elbow is maintained by the interaction between the olecranon of the ulna and the trochlea of the humerus. This stability is crucial for proper functioning and movement of the upper limb.

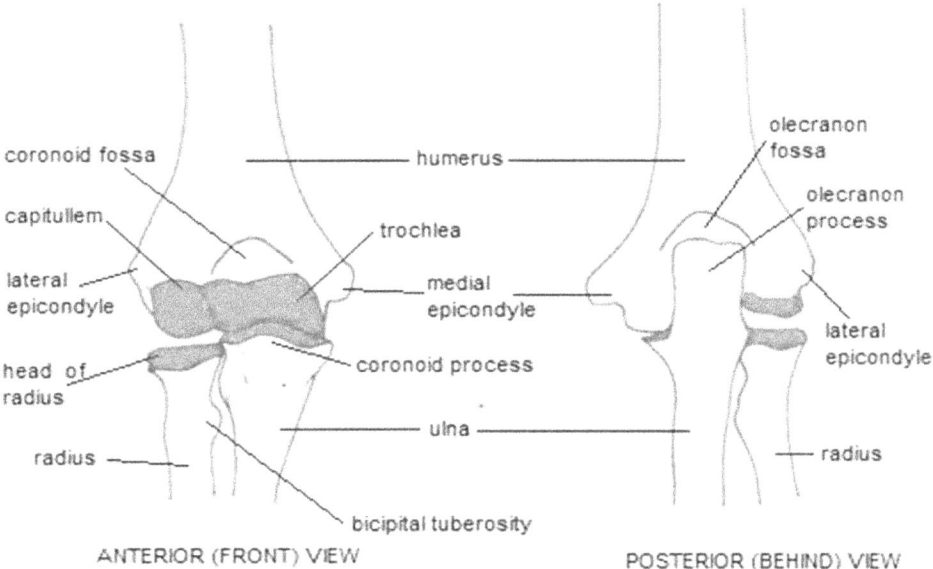

Causes of Referred pain at the elbow
- Myocardial infarction
- Cervical root lesions

- Thoracic outlet syndrome
- Sub deltoid bursitis
- Carpal tunnel syndrome – retrograde pain
- Psychogenic pain

Movements of Elbow

- 1. Flexion 140° – 150°
- 2. Extension 0 (neutral)
- 3. Supination 75° - 85°
- 4. Pronation 45° – 80°

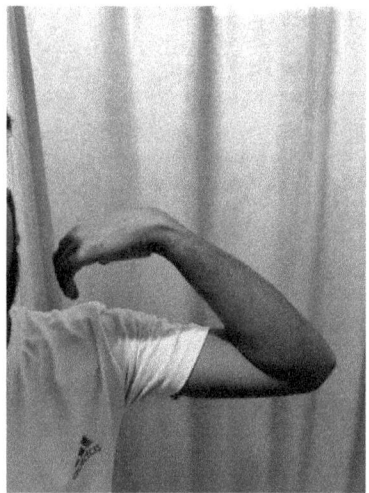

Flexion

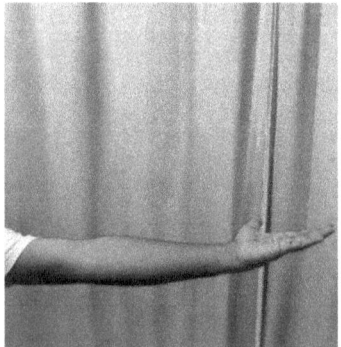

Extension

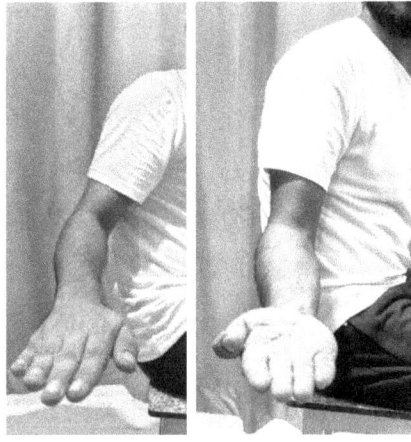

Pronation   Supination

EXAMINATION OF INJURIES ELBOW JOINT

In the examination of injuries, the **inspection** phase involves assessing attitude, swelling, and deformity. Here's a specific focus on attitude and carrying angle:

1. Attitude:

a. In Front: - Check the carrying angle in the anatomical position.

Carrying angle decreased –**cubitus varus** deformity (gunstock deformity- seen in supracondylar fracture of the humerus)

Carrying angle increased – **cubitus valgus** deformity. The carrying angle should always be compared with the opposite elbow.

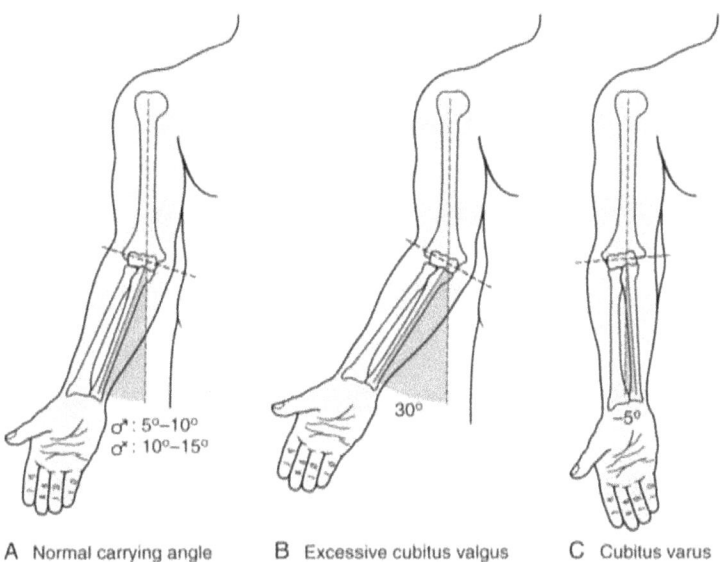

A Normal carrying angle   B Excessive cubitus valgus   C Cubitus varus

b. From Behind:
- Focus on the position of the olecranon.
- Observe whether the mid-posterior line of the arm passes through the olecranon process.

c. From the Side:
- Note the anteroposterior broadening of the elbow.
- This observation provides valuable information about the overall alignment and structure of the elbow joint.

2. Swelling:
- A significant amount of swelling may be present.
- Note the specific site of swelling, as this can provide clues about the nature and extent of the injury.

3. Deformity:
- Observe any obvious deformity.
- The presence of deformity can be crucial in diagnosing the type of injury and may guide further investigations.

Palpation

1. Local bony tenderness
2. Local bony irregularity
3. Displacement
4. Unnatural mobility
5. Crepitus
6. Tenderness

During the palpation phase of the examination of the elbow, attention is directed towards specific bony structures. These include:

Lower part of the humerus

Head and neck of the radius

Upper part of the ulna

Additionally, three key relative bony points are focused on:

- **Olecranon**
- **Medial epicondyle**
- **Lateral epicondyle**

An interesting observation is made regarding the positioning of these three bony points during different elbow states:

- In the Flexed Elbow:
- The olecranon, medial epicondyle, and lateral epicondyle form a triangle.
- In the Extended Elbow:
- The same three bony points align to form a horizontal straight line.

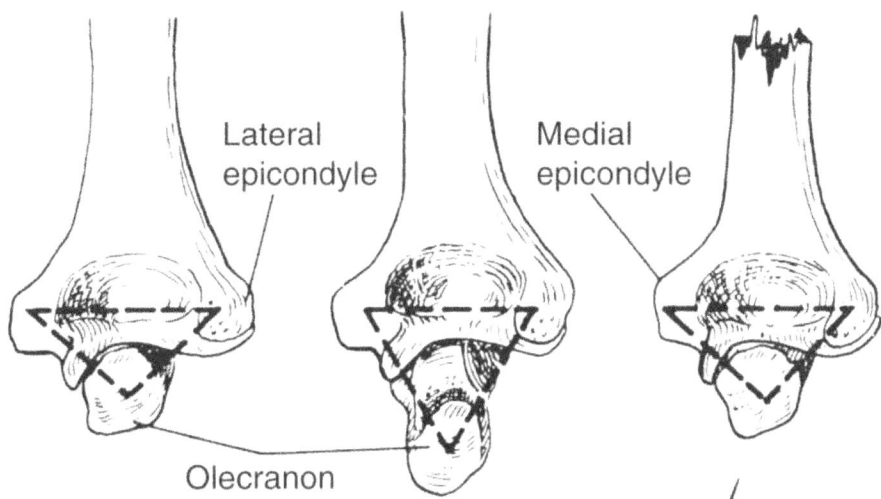

The description provides insights into the significance of pain during the springing or squeezing of the lower end of the radius and ulna:

Pain in Springing (Squeezing):

- Pain experienced during the springing or squeezing of the lower end of the radius and ulna may suggest a fracture at the upper end.
- It is noted that fractures of the head of the radius are more common in adults.
- Conversely, fractures of the neck of the radius are more common in children.

3. Measurements: The measurements taken from the angle of the acromion to the lateral epicondyle and from the lateral epicondyle to the radial styloid process are clinical assessments that provide important information about the elbow joint:

Angle of the Acromion to Lateral Epicondyle:

- Shortening in this measurement can be indicative of a supracondylar fracture of the humerus.

Lateral Epicondyle to Radial Styloid Process:

- Shortening in this measurement may suggest a posterior dislocation of the elbow.

4. Movements

When examining movements in the elbow joint, it's crucial to consider specific nuances for accurate assessment:

Supination and Pronation in Flexed Elbow:

- Supination and pronation should always be checked with the elbow flexed. This precaution is important to avoid any unintended rotation of the humerus during the assessment.

Injury to the Upper End of the Radius:

- In cases of injury to the upper end of the radius, it's noted that flexion and extension movements can still be performed.
- However, supination and pronation may be limited or arrested due to pain. Pain during these rotational movements can indicate damage or injury to the upper part of the radius.

VERY IMPORTANT:

Checking vascular and neurological status is an integral part of the examination when assessing injuries. Specific assessments for different nerves are crucial to identify potential deficits:

Vascular Assessment:

- **Always check the radial pulse** to ensure there is no vascular damage due to injury. The presence or absence of a radial pulse provides information about the vascular status in the affected limb.

Neurological Assessment:

- Median Nerve:
- **Check thumb abduction.**
- Radial Nerve:
- **Check metacarpophalangeal joint extension**.
- Ulnar Nerve:
- **Check finger abduction and adduction**.

These neurological assessments are valuable for identifying nerve-specific deficits and guiding appropriate intervention in the case of injuries or trauma.

In the acute phase of injury, especially around the elbow joint, it is recommended to avoid certain interventions to prevent complications such as post-traumatic ossification or myositis ossificans. Specifically:

Forcible Massage:

- Forceful or aggressive massage of the affected area should be avoided. Excessive pressure or manipulation may exacerbate inflammation, disrupt the healing process, and potentially contribute to the formation of abnormal bony tissue.

Hot Application:

- While hot applications can sometimes be beneficial for pain relief and relaxation, extreme caution is advised in the acute phase. Excessive heat can potentially worsen inflammation and may contribute to complications like ossification.

Passive Stretching:

- Passive stretching, particularly if done forcefully, should be avoided during the acute phase. Aggressive stretching can increase the risk of further injury and may contribute to the development of abnormal tissue.

While explaining Koorparasandhi vislesha, dalhana is commenting that for reduction purposes only it's suggested to manipulate the elbow in an acute phase.

सन्ध्यस्थनो मार्गोपलम्भार्थं मार्जनं विधेयम् (su chi 3)

Investigations

The recommended views for X-rays of the elbow joint include:

- Anteroposterior View
- Lateral View

For individuals up to 16 years of age, there is a specific recommendation:

- Bilateral View of Elbow:
- If necessary, bilateral views of the elbow may be advised. This involves obtaining X-rays of both elbows for comparison.

Additional points

Specific elbow injuries:

Posterior Dislocation of the Elbow:

- Commonly occurs in adults.
- May be associated with a coronoid fracture.
- Typically associated with lateral displacement i.e. posterolateral

Subluxation of the Head of the Radius:

- Occurs in a child below 5 years, (most common-2-5 years) often due to sudden pulling by the wrist.
- Characterized by an attitude where the elbow is in slight flexion and pronation.

- Reduction is applied by holding the head of radius with thumb of one hand, with the other hand, forceful supination of forearm and radial deviation of wrist is done.

Supracondylar Fracture of Humerus:

- In this fracture, the lower fragment is displaced backward with angulation.
- There is a potential risk of injury to the brachial artery, leading to complications such as Volkmann's ischemic contracture, cubitus varus deformity, and mal-union.

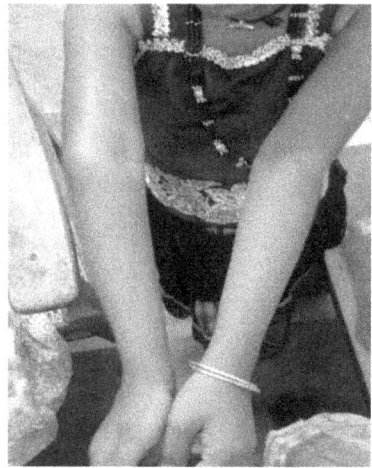

Cubitus varus or gunstock deformity of right elbow in a 12 year old girl followed by supracondylar fracture of humerus

Monteggia Fracture:

- Involves a fracture of the upper third of the ulna.
- Accompanied by dislocation of the superior radio-ulnar joint.

T and Y-Shaped Fracture:

- Commonly seen in adults.
- Presents with a swollen elbow that is notably wide.
- Movement is extremely painful and restricted.

Fracture of Medial and Lateral Condyle:

- Seen in children.
- Characterized by swelling on the affected side and tenderness

Fracture of Capitulum and Olecranon:

- In a fracture of the capitulum, typically seen in adults, there is tenderness at the fracture site.
- Flexion is extremely painful, but extension is still possible.

- In a fracture of the olecranon, a direct fall on the point of the elbow is a common cause, sometimes resulting in a displaced fracture.

Fracture of Head and Neck of Radius:

- Radius neck fractures often affect children.
- In neck fractures, patients can typically flex and extend the elbow, but supination and pronation are painful and restricted.
- Head of radius fractures, more common in adults, allow for flexion and extension with relatively little pain. However, there may be limitations or discomfort in supination and pronation movements.

EXAMINATION OF PATHOLOGY ELBOW JOINT

When examining pathology related to the elbow joint, the process involves a thorough assessment that includes consideration of the patient's history and a series of observations.

A. Inspection:

Position:

- Observe the general position of the elbow, paying attention to the carrying angle.
- In the case of effusion, the elbow may assume a semi-flexed position.

Swelling:

- Presence of swelling may indicate various conditions:
- Olecranon bursitis, characterized by swelling over the olecranon.
- Slight swelling in front of the elbow could be indicative of bicipitoradial bursitis.

Muscular Wasting:

- Assess for any signs of muscular wasting around the elbow joint.

B. Palpation:

Local Temperature:

- Increased local temperature may be observed in conditions such as acute arthritis, olecranon bursitis, and bicipitoradial bursitis.

Localized Tenderness:

- Tenderness can be assessed through palpation and may be a significant finding in conditions like lateral epicondylitis (tennis elbow) and medial epicondylitis (golfer's elbow).

Bony Components:

- Carefully palpate the bony components of the elbow to identify any tenderness or irregularities.

Swelling:
- Palpate to locate and assess the characteristics of any swelling present in the region.

C. Movements – compare both elbows

Additional points

Acute and Chronic Arthritis:
- Acute arthritis is characterized by pain and often leads to joint effusion
- Chronic arthritis is relatively uncommon in the elbow joint.

Lateral epicondylitis - Cozen's Test:
- In the evaluation of lateral epicondylitis (tennis elbow), Cozen's test is commonly employed.
- During Cozen's test, the patient is asked to dorsiflex or extend their clenched fist against resistance.

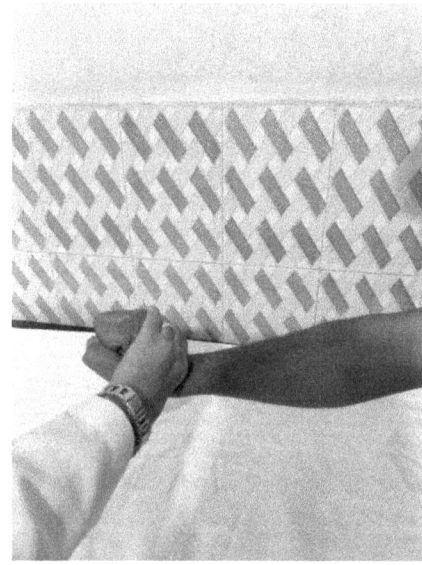

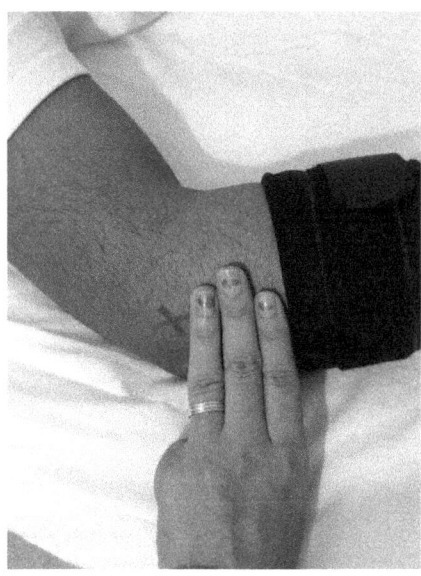

Tennis Elbow Band:

- For pain relief in lateral epicondylitis (tennis elbow), a tennis elbow band (support) is advised. It is recommended to wear the band three fingers' distance distal to the affected lateral epicondyle during activities. This band may help alleviate pain and provide support during movements.

Medial epicondylitis - Reverse Cozen's Test:

- In the assessment of medial epicondylitis (golfer's elbow), the reverse Cozen's test is performed.
- During this test, the patient is asked to flex their elbow against resistance.

Bicipitoradial Bursitis:

- Bicipitoradial bursitis is caused by repeated throwing of the ball and is characterized by pain over the insertion of the biceps muscle. This condition often results from overuse or strain on the biceps tendon.

Elbow Tunnel Syndrome:

- Elbow tunnel syndrome involves the entrapment of the ulnar nerve just beneath the medial epicondyle.
- Tinel's sign, which is a tingling sensation or "pins and needles" felt when tapping over the affected area, may be positive. This sign is indicative of nerve irritation or compression.

POSTERIOR DISLOCATION OF ELBOW JOINT

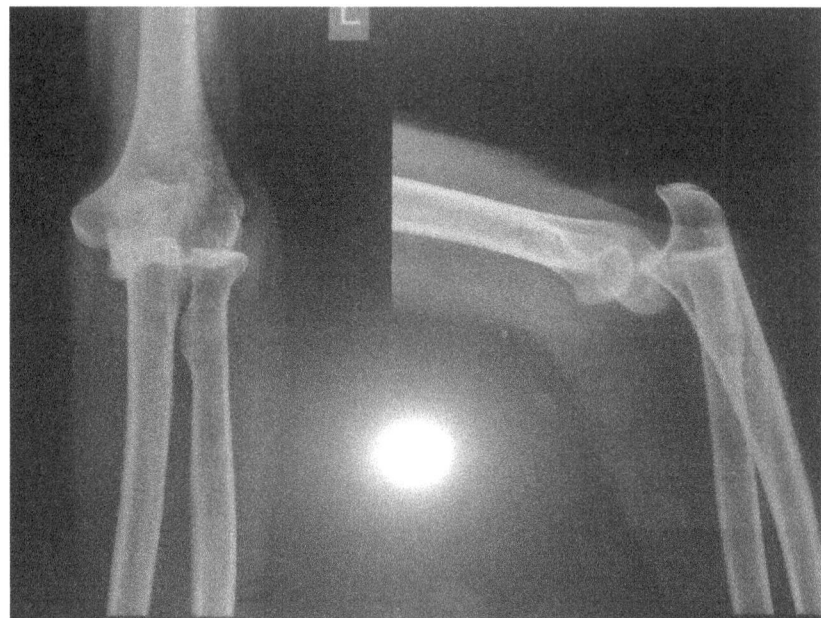

A patient comes in with a history of fall on an outstretched hand and the patient is not able to attempt any movements of the affected elbow. On inspection itself, it's possible to visualise the olecranon process of the ulna displaced posteriorly. The patient's attitude is a flexed elbow supported with the opposite hand. There will be intense pain due to the dislocation. On x-ray, it's visible that the olecranon process of the ulna along with the head of the radius is displaced posteriorly or posterolaterally to the lower end of the humerus.

There will be obvious marked deformity and pain and the patient is not able to attempt any movements. To distinguish it from the supracondylar fracture of the humerus it's better to follow a simple technique: the measurement taken from the angle of the acromion to lateral epicondyle and from lateral epicondyle to the radial styloid process. In supracondylar fracture of the humerus which is very common in children the measurement taken from the angle of the acromion (where the spine of scapula becomes an acromion process) to lateral epicondyle is shortened. In Posterior dislocation of the elbow the measurement taken from lateral epicondyle to radial styloid process is shortened. In an x-ray, it's possible to distinguish both the injuries. Always check the distal sensation, radial pulse, neurological examination for median, radial, and ulnar nerve at the distal extremity, and capillary refill test in this particular injury.

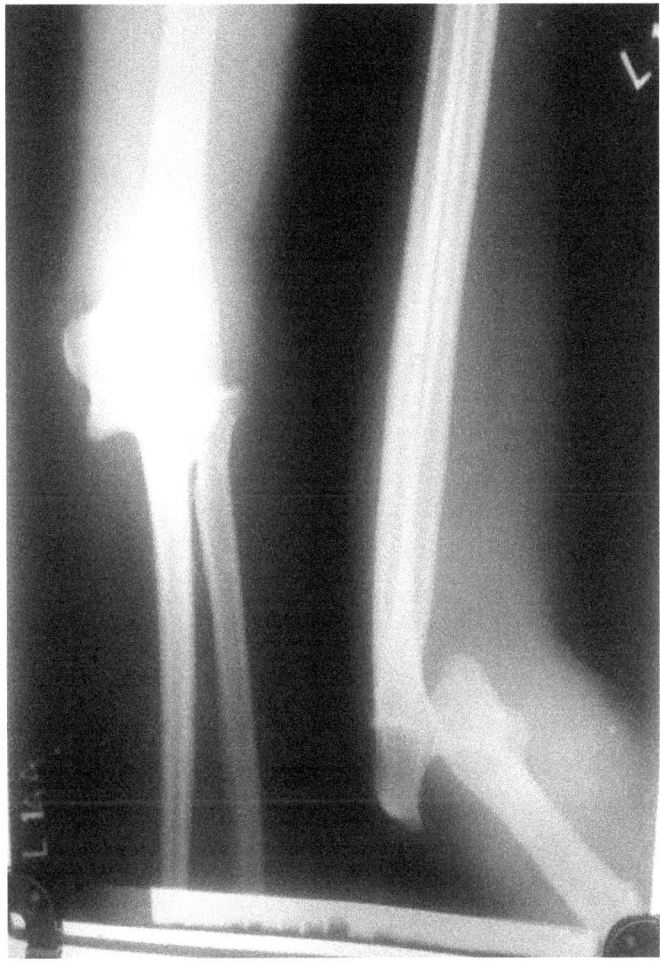

posterior dislocation of elbow

Reduction method

- Support the olecranon process with one hand, posterolaterally (**angushtena anumarjana**)
- Extension of the elbow with mild traction by holding on the distal end of the affected hand with the surgeon's other hand (**prasarana**). By this method, reduction is complete.
- Flexion of the elbow is made (**aakunchana**)
- In a ninety-degree flexed elbow, immobilization is advisable for 3 weeks. Either an above elbow half cast or an aluminium splinted bandage from the end of the deltoid muscle to the metacarpophalangeal joint is done.
- Sneha seka (**after the removal of bandage as rehabilitation**)

In Ayurveda, Acharya Sushruta mentioned,

कौपरं तु तथा सन्धिमङ्गुष्ठेनानुमार्जयेत् |
अनुमृज्य ततः सन्धिं पीडयेत् कूर्पराच्च्युतम् ||३२||
प्रसार्याकुञ्चयेच्चैनं स्नेहसेकं च दापयेत् (SU.CHI 3)

Angushtena anumarjanam means supporting the olecranon. The second is prasarana, extension, and the third is akunchanam, flexion. Sneha sekam is advised and it should be done after 3 weeks of immobilization. In all dislocations, the healing of the joint capsule happens by 3 weeks of immobilization. Elbow joints which are prone to stiffness become stiff by 3 weeks of immobilization. So it's better to use Sneha seka, after removal of the bandage. Dhara with dhanyamla followed by sneha dhara with asavenna is beneficial to regain functional movements.

As the elbow is more prone to stiffness, passive stretching, hot application, and massage should be avoided in the initial phase. The same is explained by dalhana in the current context.

मार्गोपलम्भार्थं मार्जनं विधेयम् (SU.CHI 3) -dalhana tika

After reduction on x-ray, it's possible to see a complete reduction.

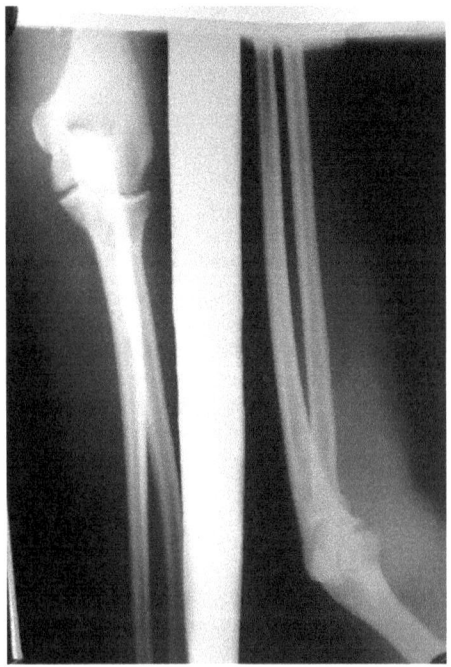

Bandage

First, apply a stockinette in a 90-degree flexed elbow. Then apply a top ban or compressed cotton. After applying compressed cotton, 15 cm 12-layered POP is applied as half cast from the metacarpophalangeal joint up to the distal end of the deltoid. It's followed by 10 cm 4-layered POP is utilised as an additional stir-up and is applied over the medial and lateral aspect of the forearm and then pop is fixed with a wet gauze. It should be re-bandaged in a gap of 7 days. The patient should be advised to do rehabilitation of fingers and shoulder from the first day of bandage.

After 3 weeks of immobilization, the bandage is removed and rehabilitation for elbow and wrist should be started. If there is swelling, lepa or upanaha with nagaradi is advisable. If there is no swelling, it's advisable to start dhara with dhanyamla followed by asavenna and lavana, amla rasa taila. Dhara or Seka shall be advised for 7 days. If the complete Range of movements is not regained, it's better to continue dhara (seka) for an additional 7 days. By 21 days of rehabilitation, it's possible to regain the complete movements of the elbow.

6. WRIST JOINT AND HAND

Applied Anatomy

Wrist:

Bones:

- The wrist is composed of eight carpal bones arranged in two rows (proximal and distal). These bones articulate with the radius and ulna of the forearm and the metacarpal bones of the hand.

Carpal Bones:

- The proximal row of carpal bones consists of scaphoid, lunate, triquetrum, and pisiform. (from lateral to medial)
- The distal row includes trapezium, trapezoid, capitate, and hamate.

Joints:

- The wrist joint, or radiocarpal joint, is where the radius articulates with the proximal row of carpal bones. Various ligaments contribute to stability.

Movements:

- Flexion, extension, abduction, and adduction occur at the wrist joint. Circumduction, a circular movement, is also possible.

Hand:

Metacarpal Bones:

- The five metacarpal bones connect the wrist to the fingers and provide a stable base for hand function.

Metacarpophalangeal (MCP) and Interphalangeal (IP) Joints:

- The MCP and IP joints allow flexion and extension.

Thumb Carpometacarpal (CMC) Joint:

- The thumb has a unique joint at the base (CMC joint) that allows a wide range of movements, including opposition and rotation.

TFCC stands for Triangular Fibrocartilage Complex, and it is a structure in the wrist that plays a crucial role in maintaining stability and facilitating smooth movement.

Functions of TFCC:

Stability:

- It stabilizes the ulna and radius bones during gripping and rotational movements.

Load Transmission:
- The TFCC helps distribute forces and loads across the wrist joint, preventing excessive wear and tear.

Smooth Movement:
- It allows for smooth and coordinated movement between the forearm and the hand.

TFCC Tear:
- Tears in the fibrocartilage can occur due to trauma, overuse, or degeneration.

TFCC Injury:
- Injuries may result from falls on an outstretched hand, repetitive stress, or degenerative changes over time.

Diagnosis of TFCC injuries typically involves clinical evaluation.

Clinical diagnosis done with eliciting positive fovea sign, tenderness just beneath ulnar styloid process. Forceful ulnar deviation and supination reproduces pain. 3- 6 weeks of immobilization is needed in acute TFCC injury.

Movements

1. Flexion – 60°
2. Extension - 70°
3. Adduction (ulnar deviation) - 35°
4. Abduction (radial deviation) - 25°
5. MetaCarpophalangeal joint - 0-90°
6. Proximal Interphalangeal joint - 0-100°
7. Distal Interphalangeal joint – 0-80°

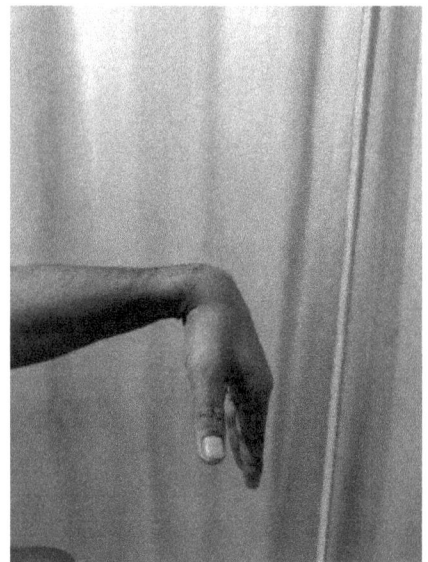

Flexion

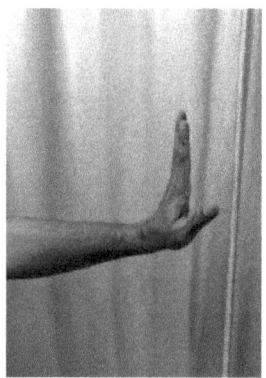

Extension (dorsiflexion)

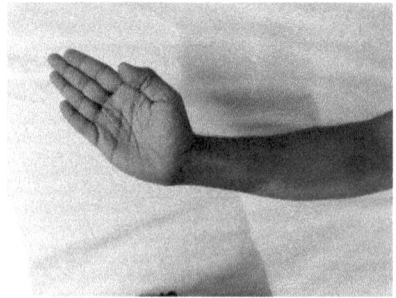

Radial deviation (Abduction)

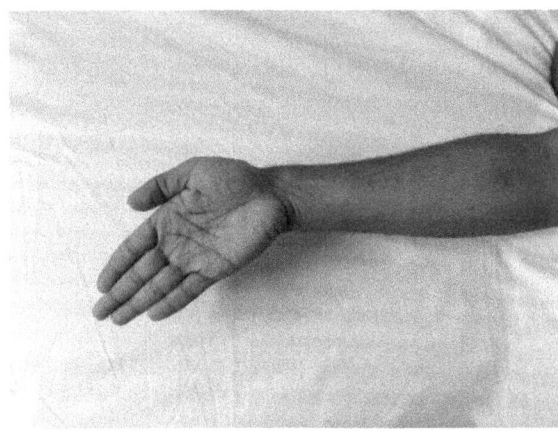 Ulnar deviation (Adduction)

EXAMINATION OF INJURY WRIST JOINT AND HAND

Inspection

Deformity

1. Dinner fork deformity – Colles' fracture
2. Slight anterior projection at wrist – dislocation of the lunate
3. Lateral projection at the base of first MetaCarpal – Bennet's fracture
4. Dorsal subluxation with prominence of lower end of ulna–madelung's deformity
5. Persistent flexion of terminal phalanx – mallet finger
6. Line of knuckles not on normal line on clenched fist – metacarpal fracture

Palpation

1. Local bony tenderness
2. Bony irregularity
3. Displacement
4. Unnatural mobility
5. Crepitus

a. lower third of radius – lower third of radius is smoothly concave in front. In Colles' fracture, dorsal displacement is present. In Galeazzi fracture, there is a fracture of the lower third of the radius with inferior dislocation of the radio-ulnar joint.

Springing the radius – squeezing the upper end of the ulna and radius will elicit pain at the site of the lower end of the radius fracture

b. the lower third of the ulna–ulna is subcutaneous and can palpate full length. In Colles' fracture, the styloid process of the ulna is fractured in 50% of cases.

c. palpation of two styloid processes – normally the radial styloid process is 1 cm lower than that of the ulna. In Colles' fracture, both remain in the same line.

d. carpal bones – palpation of the scaphoid is important and is palpated at the anatomical snuff box with the wrist bent medially to expose the bone for palpation. Check tenderness of scaphoid tubercle if anatomical snuff-box tenderness is elicited. The special view for scaphoid is WRIST PA with Ulnar deviation

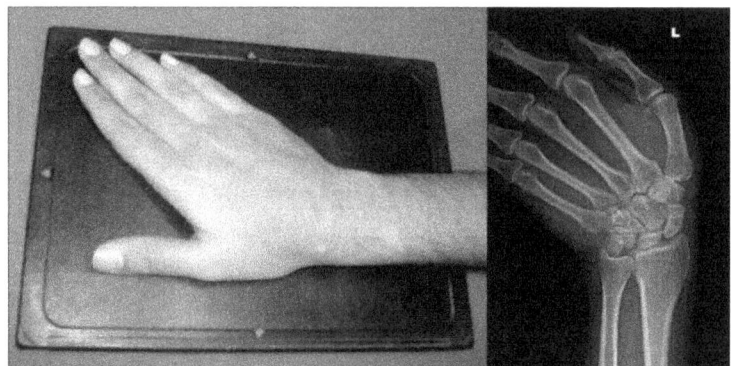

e. metacarpals and phalanges – palpate the full length of metacarpals and phalanges.

Metacarpals – springing or traction at phalanges shall be done

Phalanges – traction elicits tenderness at the fracture site

Movements

movement of the affected part will be painful and limited

Complications

In **scaphoid fracture** through the waist (middle), there is a chance of non–union and avascular necrosis of the proximal fragment of the scaphoid.

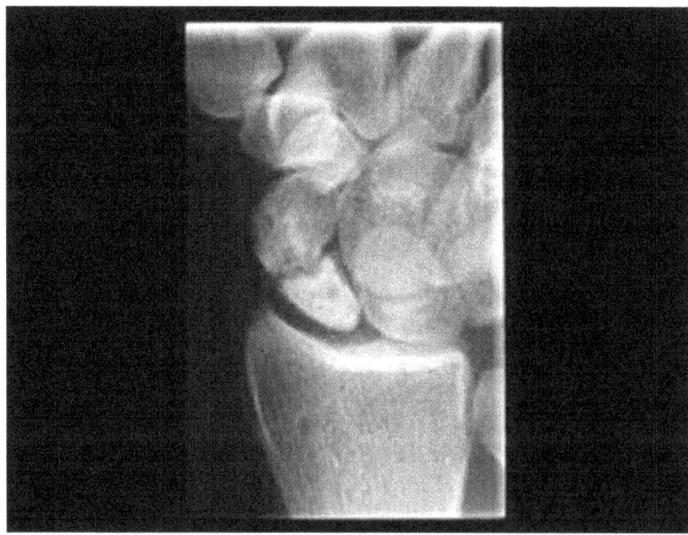

Investigations

X-ray

Wrist
- AP
- LATERAL
- SCAPHOID VIEW
- for confirmation of diagnosis and help the clinician with the reduction of displaced fragments.
- Scaphoid fracture - oblique view and views from different angles. An X-ray after 10 days (check X-ray) should be taken, if needed.

Differential Diagnosis

Smith's Fracture:

- Mechanism: Fall on the dorsum of the palmar-flexed wrist.
- Presentation: Anterior displacement of distal radius.
- It's difficult to manage conservatively as reduction in closed manipulative reduction (CMR) may not be perfect on check X-ray

Chauffeur's Fracture:

- Occurrence: Common in road traffic accidents (RTA).
- Characteristics: Transverse fracture line, often undisplaced.
- Possible to follow conservative management.

Galeazzi Fracture:

- Definition: Fracture dislocation of the lower end of the radius with inferior radio-ulnar dislocation.
- Always require surgical management.

Madelung's Deformity:

- Description: Dorsal subluxation of the lower end of the ulna.

Scaphoid Fracture:

- Patient Profile: Usually young adults.
- Mechanism: Falling on an outstretched hand.
- Clinical Sign: Tenderness over the anatomical snuff box.
- Diagnosis: Check X-ray after 10 days.
- 2-3 month immobilization
- the cast should extend down up to the thumb to the level of the interphalangeal joint

Metacarpal fracture:
- Line of knuckles not on normal line on clenched fist
- 3-4 weeks immobilization should be needed with an aluminium splint (flexible to any shape) ventrally and dorsally.

Lunate and Perilunate Dislocation:
- Diagnosis: Careful palpation and lateral view X-ray
- strong traction and counter traction first
- then direct pressure over displaced bone.
- 3 weeks immobilization is needed

Bennett's Fracture Dislocation:
- Characteristics: Oblique fracture at the base of the first metacarpal along with dislocation.

Fracture and Dislocation of Metacarpals and Phalanges:
- Diagnosis: Clinical diagnosis possible, confirmed by X-ray.

Boxer's Fracture:
- Location: Fracture of the neck of the 5th metacarpal.
- Mechanism: History involves punching using a closed fist.
- traction and counter traction should be maintained till the end of the bandage
- Correction of displacement must be ensured.
- Requires 3-4 weeks immobilization up to absence of tenderness

Ulnar collateral ligament sprain
- History is direct injury to thumb
- Common in sports activities
- Bandage for 3 weeks with swasthika (figure of eight) or a thumb spica splint is found to be effective.

Mallet Finger:
- Injury: Rupture of the extensor tendon at the distal joint of the phalanx.
- Mechanism: Forced flexion of the terminal phalanx.
- Clinical Sign: Inability to extend the distal interphalangeal joint.
- Diagnosis: X-ray to rule out chip fracture of the terminal phalanx.
- Mallet splint for 6 weeks is effective.

EXAMINATION OF PATHOLOGY WRIST JOINT AND HAND

Inspection

Position:

- Rheumatoid Arthritis (RA): Ulnar deviation may be present in RA cases.

Swelling:

- Differential Diagnosis: Important to differentiate from the effusion of tendon sheaths.

Deformity:

- Rheumatoid arthritis (RA) is noted for deformities in the hand joints.

Sinus:

- Clinical Significance: The presence of a sinus may raise suspicion of TB involvement.

Palpation

Swelling:

- Fluctuation: Assess whether the swelling is fluctuant or not.

Tenderness:

- Location: Tenderness in the joint line suggests arthritis, while tenderness along the tendon indicates tenosynovitis.

Deformity:

- Palpation: Palpate the area to identify and assess the actual deformity.

Movements

Extension/Dorsiflexion:

- Position: Namaste (elbow upwards).

Flexion:

- Position: Reverse Namaste (elbow downwards).

Clinical Significance: Pain during wrist movements can be indicative of arthritis, contributing to the diagnostic evaluation.

Differential diagnosis

Acute Arthritis:

- Clinical Features:
- Pain
- Tenderness
- Effusion of the joint

Tuberculosis:

- Occurrence in Wrist:
- Rare but possible.
- Distinctive Features:
- Weakness
- Wasting
- Cold abscess
- Sinus formation

Ganglion:

- Demographics:
- Typically found in young adults.
- Characteristics:
- Painless lump
- Commonly on the dorsal aspect of the wrist

De-Quervain's disease (stenosing tenosynovitis)

- Chronic inflammation of the common sheath of tendons of abductor pollicis longus and extensor pollicis brevis.

- Often attributed to degenerative changes or unaccustomed overuse.
- Typically affects women in their forties.
- Main complaint is pain in the radial styloid process.
- Diagnostic Test: Finkelstein Test:
- Description: Involves placing the thumb in the palm, making a fist by superimposing the fingers over the thumb, and then passively pushing to the ulnar side.
- Pain is experienced over the radial styloid process during this maneuver.

Carpal Tunnel Syndrome (CTS):

- Compression neuropathy of the median nerve.
- More prevalent in women between 40-60 years.
- Pain, tingling, and numbness in the affected hand, particularly the thumb, index, and middle fingers.
- Progressive weakness and impairment of fine movements are common complaints.
- Diagnostic Test: Phalen's Sign:
- Description: The patient flexes the wrist, exacerbating symptoms within one minute.
- Result: Symptoms disappear as soon as the wrist is straightened.
- Nerve Conduction Study:
- Result: Elicits a delay in motor conduction of the median nerve at the wrist.

Note:

Systemic Conditions Screening:

- Importance: It's crucial to rule out Diabetes Mellitus and Hypothyroidism in all Carpal Tunnel Syndrome cases.
- Rationale: These systemic conditions can contribute to or exacerbate symptoms related to nerve compression.

Progression of Carpal Tunnel Syndrome (CTS):

- Stages:
- First and Second Stage: Typical symptoms like pain, tingling, and numbness.
- Third Stage: Wasting of the thenar muscles, resulting in a boat-shaped depression.
- Motor Neuron Disease (MND) Differentiation:
- **CTS: Wasting is specific to the thenar muscles (boat shaped depression), and sensory symptoms are present.**
- **MND: Entire thenar muscle wasting is observed with motor symptoms.**

Treatment

De-Quervain's, Carpal Tunnel Syndrome – pachana, modified srunga if needed, and snehana (internally)

Orthosis

- **Thumb spica splint - De-Quervain's**
- **Wrist splint – CTS**

NB. It is recommended to use orthosis for Carpal tunnel syndrome and De Quervain's tenosynovitis during rest and sleep. However, the tennis elbow band should be consistently worn during activities, and the thumb spica splint advised for ulnar collateral ligament sprain should always be worn.

CARPAL TUNNEL SYNDROME – MODIFIED SRUNGA/ALABU

Take a 10 ml syringe, use a No. 12 blade attached to the BP handle, and cut the distal end of the 10 ml syringe. After cutting the 10 ml syringe, reverse the piston to get a small area of suction to do srunga for carpal tunnel syndrome. There's a need to get a small space for suction where the median nerve is compressed, which is the cause of carpal tunnel syndrome.

Before doing the procedure, the piston is reversed and the tinel's sign is elicited. Create suction using the 10 ml syringe. Before doing the procedure always check for systemic illness. In this method, it's advisable to use a No. 12-blade or No. 18 needle to do the pricking. This procedure is found to be highly effective in grade 2 carpal tunnel syndrome. Followed by pricking, suction is done and wait for 10 min. After that, remove the suction by keeping cotton on both sides and wipe out the blood. After the procedure, check the tinel's sign. 50-80% relief will be there for the patient and the relief persists. One day bandages are kept over that area.

COLLES' FRACTURE[2]

Whenever a patient above the age of 40, falls on an outstretched hand, there is a chance of Colles' fracture (distal end of radius fracture). Colles' fracture is a fracture at the distal end of the radius within 2.5 cm from the wrist joint, with or without avulsion of the ulnar styloid process, with a characteristic deformity known as dinner fork deformity or silver fork deformity and the distal fragment displaced posteriorly or dorsally and laterally or radially.

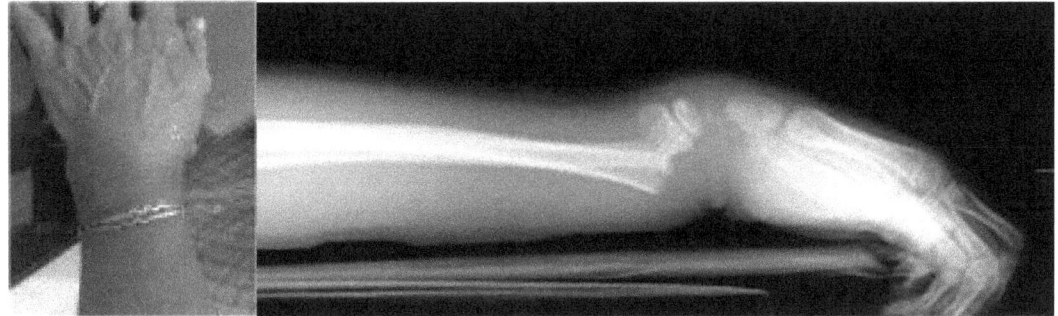

X-ray advised is Wrist AP, lateral.

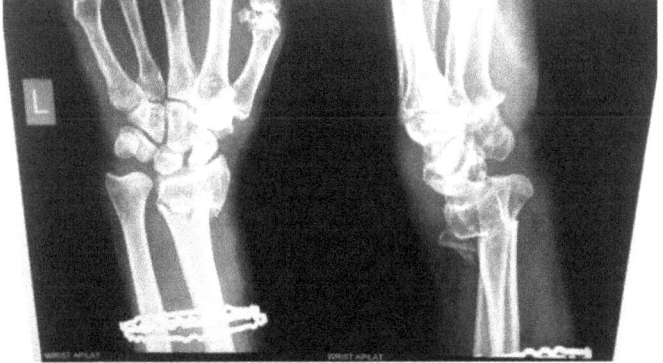

before reduction

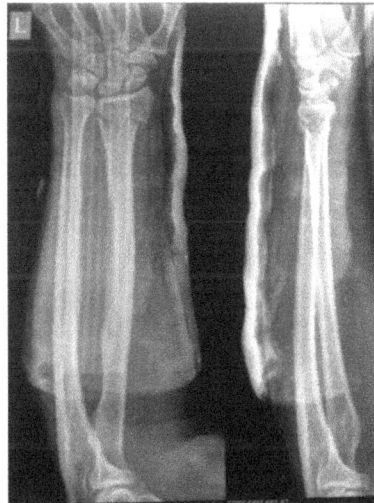

after reduction

REDUCTION AND BANDAGE

First, measure the distance from the metacarpophalangeal joint to the elbow for a below-elbow half-cast. 12 layers of 10 cm POP are taken. For each patient, the measurement will be different.

There is dorsal displacement and radial displacement in colles' fractures. For reduction, one person should give counter traction over the elbow, and the other person should hold the thumb and the other four fingers and give traction. By traction and counter traction, disimpactment of fragments will happen. The thumb of the affected hand of the patient should be towards the person who is giving traction and the other 4 fingers should be kept 90 degrees to the thumb. This position is traction with ulnar deviation. The ulnar deviation is to reduce the radial displacement. To correct the dorsal displacement we are using our thenar eminence. After supporting the proximal fragment with one thenar eminence, using the thenar eminence of the other hand the distal fragment's dorsal displacement is corrected. The radial displacement and dorsal displacement are corrected. The traction and counter traction should be maintained up to the end of the bandage. After the proper reduction, it's advisable to apply gauze from MCP to just below elbow joint initially. It's recommended to pour Murivenna into the fractured part to reduce the pitta rakta kopa in the initial phase due to the hematoma formation occurring after fracture.

Then it's better to apply a compressed cotton or top ban. The top ban should be covered 3 layers over the proximal, distal, fractured area, and joints. In all other areas, it's suggestable to provide 2 layer covering of top ban. The succeeding turn should cover two-thirds of the preceding turn. After this, application of POP over the dorsal aspect and an aluminum splint over the ventral aspect is employed. It's advisable to keep the bandage in a mild palmar flexion and ulnar deviation to avoid re-displacement. It's better to make a V-shaped slit at the distal end of the pop which will facilitate the movement of the thumb. Then fix the POP using wet gauze. It's recommended to mobilize the fingers from the first day of bandage as part of rehabilitation and to facilitate circulation. It's a better option to pour Murivenna (5ml) in between the aluminum splint and the POP, mainly over a small area ventrally, twice daily in the initial phase up to callus formation. After bandage, it's a must to apply a broad arm sling. The repeat bandage is done on the 7th day and 21st day. Whenever there is an absence of tenderness at the fracture site, mostly after 28 days, 35, or 42 days, it's better to remove the bandage and ask the patient to do rehabilitation of the wrist.

7. TEMPOROMANDIBULAR JOINT (TMJ) DISLOCATION REDUCTION METHOD

The patient came to OPD with bilateral Temporomandibular joint dislocation whose mouth is open and is unable to close. By wearing the gloves, protect the thumb with cotton packed inside the gloves, and both the thumbs are placed inside the mouth of the patient distal to molar teeth. Downward and backward pressure is given with the thumb. Other fingers are placed over the mandible for the support. By the downward and backward pressure distal to the third molar teeth, it is reduced. Immediately after the reduction, the pain is reduced and the patient can close the mouth.

In the unilateral dislocation, the reduction method is the same i.e. downward and backward pressure is to be given with the thumb.

Take a four-layered gauze piece and cut at both ends, so that it's possible to obtain a four-tailed bandage or 'khatwa' for the bandaging purpose immediately after the reduction. The right anterior tail is tied to the left posterior and the left anterior to the right posterior. Here, this is a case of oro mandibular dystonia (in QR code video) and tertiary parkinsonism, so there is a chance of recurrence of TMJ dislocation in this patient. In Ayurveda, it is advised to give nasya to strengthen the muscles around the TMJ, to avoid recurrent dislocation.

हन्वस्थिनी समानीय हनुसन्धौ विसंहते ||३९||

स्वेदयित्वा स्थिते सम्यक् पञ्चाङ्गीं वितरेद्भिषक् |

वातघ्नमधुरैः सर्पिः सिद्धं नस्ये च पूजितम् (SU CHI 3)

8. KNEE JOINT

Applied anatomy of the knee joint

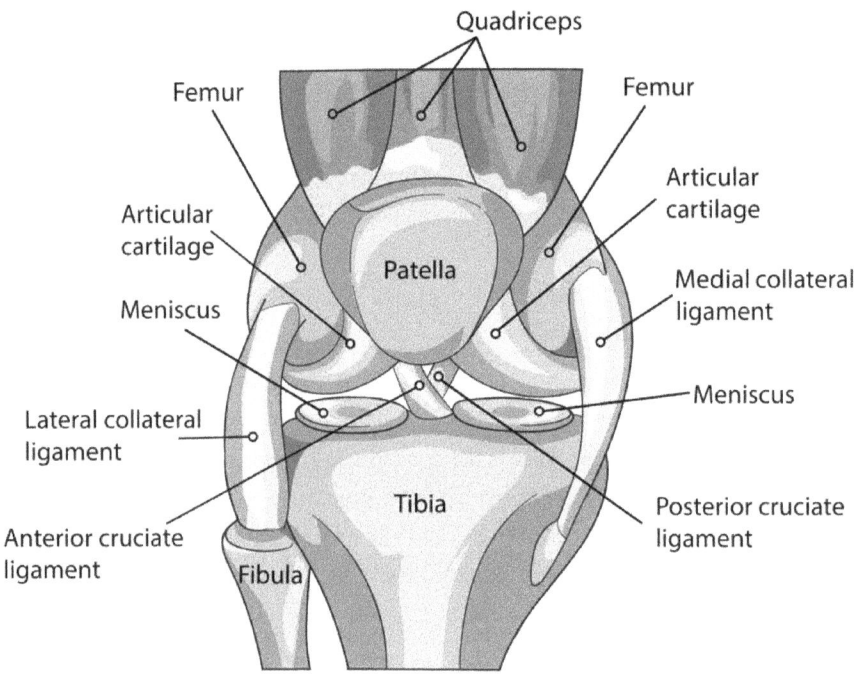

Knee Joint Components:

Tibiofemoral Joint:

- Consists of two articulations: medial and lateral.
- The medial joint is between the medial femoral condyle and medial tibial condyle.
- The lateral joint is between the lateral femoral condyle and the lateral tibial condyle.
- Prone to conditions like osteoarthritis of the knee. Commonly the medial compartment is affected.

Patellofemoral Joint:

- Articulation between the femur and patella (kneecap).
- Prone to conditions like patellofemoral syndrome and chondromalacia patella.

The knee is the largest joint in the human body.

Modified Hinge Joint:

- The knee is a modified hinge joint that primarily allows movement of flexion and extension.

Movements

- **Flexion 120-150°**
- **Extension 5-10°**
- **Internal rotation (in 90° flexed) 10°** -not relevant
- **External rotation 30-40°** --not relevant

<u>Ligaments of knee</u>

***Intracapsular** ligament includes

1. ACL (Anterior Cruciate Ligament)
2. PCL (Posterior Cruciate Ligament)
3. Transverse Ligament - These connect both the medial and lateral meniscus

***Extracapsular** ligament includes

1. Patellar ligament (in between patella and tibial tuberosity)
2. MCL (Medial Collateral Ligament)
3. LCL (Lateral Collateral Ligament)

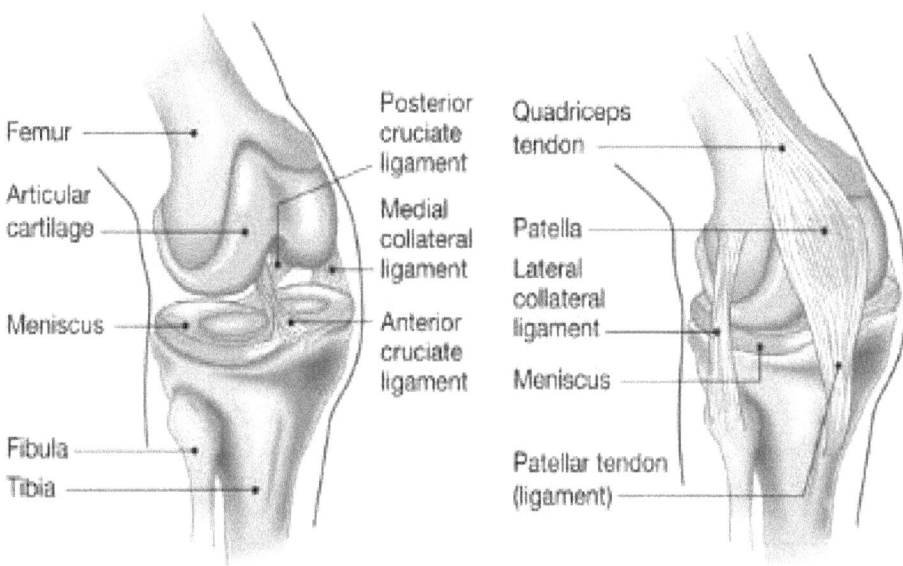

The knee joint

- The patellar tendon connects the patella and tibial tuberosity.

- The meniscus helps to absorb shock and is attached to the tibia; the medial meniscus is firmly attached to the tibia while the lateral meniscus is loosely attached. The periphery of both menisci are vascular but the body of both menisci are avascular. So whenever a tear occurs at the body of the meniscus it won't be healed. But in the case of the periphery of the meniscus, healing is possible.
- The anterior cruciate ligament connects the anterior tibial plateau and lateral femoral condyle
- The posterior cruciate ligament connects the posterior tibial plateau and medial femoral condyle. Both cruciate ligament crosses each other
- The lateral collateral ligament connects the lateral femoral condyle to the head of the fibula
- The medial collateral ligament lies close to the medial meniscus. But there is no connection between the lateral collateral ligament and the lateral meniscus. So whenever an injury occurs to the medial collateral ligament there is a chance for injury to the medial meniscus too.

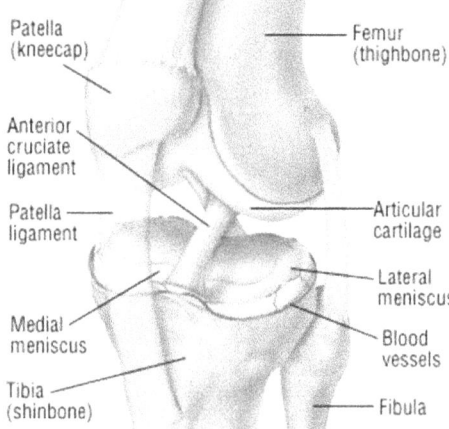

- The anterior cruciate ligament is more prone to injury than the posterior cruciate ligament and in the meniscus, the medial meniscus is more prone to injury. Medial Collateral Ligament (MCL) is more prone to injury, when compared to Lateral Collateral Ligament (LCL).
- When Medial collateral ligament, Medial meniscus, and Anterior cruciate ligament tear occur simultaneously; it is known as unhappy triad which requires a surgical reference.

The pes anserine consists of the conjoined tendons of the sartorius, gracilis, and semitendinosus muscles. Pes anserine bursa is prone to bursitis due to direct injury or **Repeated Strain Injury (RSI)**. Pes anserine Bursitis is also seen in osteoarthritis patients.

Examination for pes anserine bursitis

- In a prone position, flex the knee up to ninety degrees and ask the patient to further flex the knee joint against resistance. The patient feels typical pain over the pes anserine area.

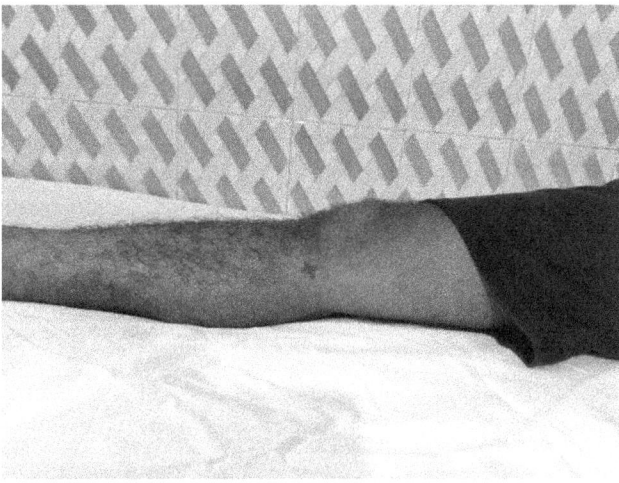

Functions of ligament

- Medial collateral: prevents medial opening up
- Lateral collateral: prevents lateral opening up
- Anterior cruciate: prevents anterior translation of the tibia on the femur
- Posterior cruciate: prevents posterior translation of the tibia on the femur

POSTERO-LATERAL CORNER (PLC) OF KNEE

THE POSTERO-LATERAL CORNER of the knee consists of

- Fibular collateral ligament
- Popliteus muscle
- Popliteo-fibular ligament

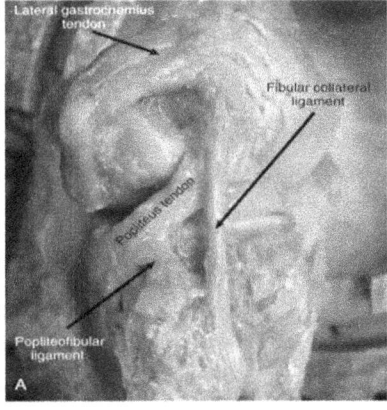
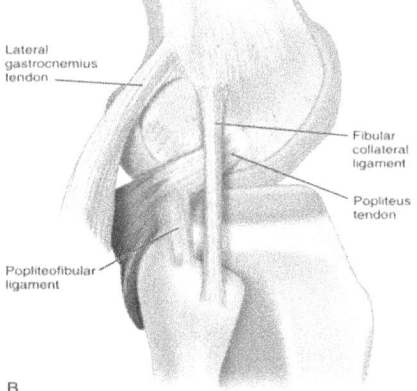

Bursa around the knee joint

*Suprapatellar bursa (situated in suprapatellar pouch)

*Prepatellar bursa (situated in between patella and skin)

* Infrapatellar bursa (seen in medial and lateral side of patellar tendon and is divided into superficial and deep)

* Pes anserine bursa

*Semimembranosus bursa

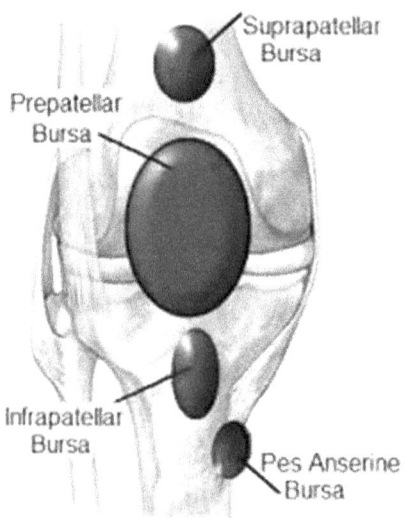

Whenever there is friction between the patella and skin continuously due to kneeling it causes prepatellar bursitis which is commonly known as housemaid's knee. When there is friction between the skin and tibia, it causes Infrapatellar bursitis and is known as clergyman's knee (clergyman means priest; occurs due to continuous kneeling as part of prayer).

Extensor apparatus of the knee

From proximal to distal

- Quadriceps muscle
- Quadriceps tendon
- Patella with patellar retinaculum on the sides
- Patellar tendon
- Complete Tear of Quadriceps or Patellar Tendon:
    - When there is a complete tear of the quadriceps or patellar tendon, or an avulsion fracture of the patella, the patient may experience an inability to perform knee extension.

- Assessing Extensor Apparatus Patency:
    - The patency of the extensor apparatus is checked by the patient's ability to perform the active straight leg raise (SLR).
- Significance of Active SLR:
    - If active SLR is possible after the injury, it indicates that the extensor apparatus is partially intact, and conservative management may be considered.
- Indication for Conservative Management:
    - If active SLR is possible, conservative management may be considered for recovery.
- Surgical Reference:
    - If active SLR is not possible, it suggests a more severe injury, and the condition may be considered "asadhya vyadhi"
    - In such cases, surgical intervention is often necessary, and the patient should be referred for surgical evaluation and management.

This clinical approach emphasizes the importance of assessing the functional capacity of the extensor apparatus through active SLR to guide treatment decisions, whether conservative or surgical, for optimal patient outcomes.

Note:
- knee dislocation won't happen without high-energy trauma which requires surgical correction.
- In patellar subluxation it's advisable to do conservative management with closed manipulative reduction.
- No reduction is needed in a ligament tear. Never attempt forceful manipulation in ligament injuries of the knee. It may lead to further complications.
- Spine and hip examination is a must for knee joint pain presentation. Because whenever there is an L3 lesion it causes quadriceps and knee pain.
- In avascular necrosis pain starts from the hip and radiates towards the medial side of the knee and the patient presents with pain over the medial side of knee. So the range of motion and specific movements of the hip should be checked.

NB. **Osteoid osteoma** and knee pain: Lesions in the **proximal femur, the lesser trochanter, and the femoral neck** can also be a cause of **knee pain.**

Palpation of patellar ligament.
- In Johannson Larsen syndrome seen in the age group of 10-14, the patellar ligament pulls down the patella and the distal end of the patella is painful.

- In Osgood Schlatter syndrome pain is felt in the tibial tuberosity, the patellar ligament pulls up the tibial tuberosity and the age group affected is 14-16
- In the age group 16-30, there is a chance of patellar tendonitis which is very common in runners.
- It's advisable to palpate the patellar ligament in a 90° flexed knee joint.
- In Johansen Larsen syndrome, Osgood Schlatter syndrome, and patellar tendonitis; the clinical examination is - Ask the patient to extend knee against resistance, which causes pain in distal patella, tibial tuberosity and patellar tendon respectively.

Palpation of Medial joint line
- Just medial to the patellar tendon is the medial joint line
- It's possible to palpate the medial joint line in between the medial femoral condyle and medial tibial condyle.
- On palpation, if tenderness is present on the medial joint line, it may be due to osteoarthritis. If it is after an injury it may be due to medial meniscus injury. If tenderness present without injury that may be due to horizontal tear (most common tear of meniscus and are degenerative tears) or radial tear to meniscus

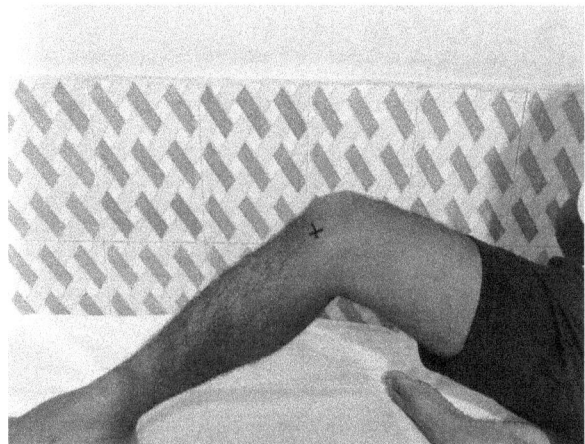

Palpation of the lateral joint line

It is lateral to the patellar ligament in between the lateral femoral condyle and the lateral tibial condyle. Lateral joint line pain may be elicited in lateral meniscal injury.

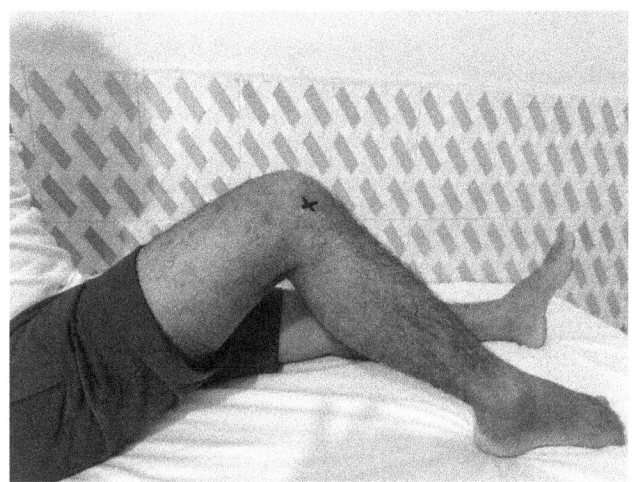

KNEE JOINT INJURY
ANTERIOR CRUCIATE LIGAMENT INJURY (ACL)

- Sudden changes in direction while running, errors in landing ground after jumping, history of hyperextension are the main causes of Anterior cruciate ligament injury.
- Immediately after the injury there will be giving way to the affected knee.
- When compared to meniscal tear knee joint effusion will be faster in Anterior cruciate ligament injury. The patient is not able to continue the activities after Anterior cruciate ligament tear

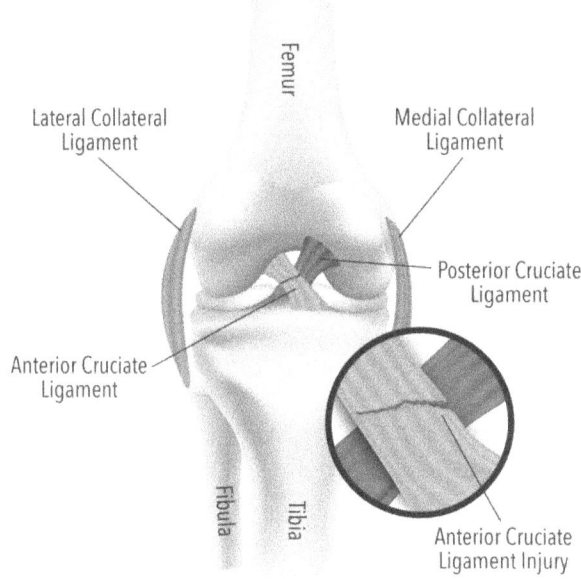

Anterior Cruciate Ligament Injury

Clinical examination

Lachman's Test for ACL Tear:

- Patient Positioning:
- Knee flexed to 20-30°.
- Examiner holds the upper end of the tibia, with the thumb on the tibial tuberosity and four other fingers on the posterior aspect.
- Lower end of the femur is fixed anteriorly, ensuring the hamstring is relaxed.
- Test Execution:
- Simultaneously pull the tibia anteriorly and push the femur posteriorly.
- Assess for anterior translation of the tibia.
- Comparison with Drawer Test:
- More sensitive and confirmatory than the Drawer Test.

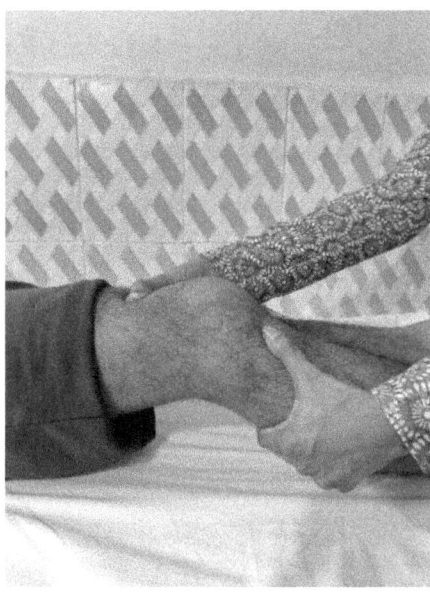

Anterior Drawer Test for ACL Tear:
- Patient Positioning:
- Knee flexed to 90°.
- Examiner sits on the foot to stabilize it.
- Grasp the upper end of the tibia just distal to the joint line.
- Test Execution:
- Pull the tibia anteriorly.
- Assess for anterior translation of the tibia compared to the lower end of the femur.
- Note the presence or absence of a tough endpoint.
- Interpretation:
- In normal conditions, there is mild movement with a tough endpoint.
- Complete ACL tear results in no tough endpoint, and there is more anterior translation of the tibia.
- Caution:
- Ensure the hamstring is relaxed before performing the test.

Management of acute knee ligament injuries (internal derangement of the knee, **IDK**)

Primary management of the ligament injury is **immobilization** above the knee cast in the **Z** position. A posterior cast should be applied in the 30° flexed knee joint and the foot is kept in 90° i.e. dorsiflexion of the foot. Whenever the pain subsides, the bandage should be removed and a simple figure of eight bandages or swastika bandha is applied and then start rehabilitation.

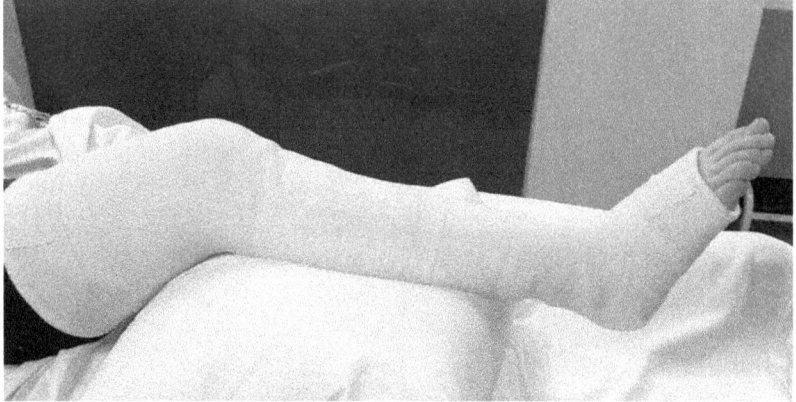

Instead of a knee cast, it's advisable to use a knee immobilizer up to the period of immobilization. The knee immobilizer can be changed to a hinged knee brace whenever the condition improves. The hinged knee brace allows 45° flexion and then rehabilitation should be started.

For a grade I injury, a simple bandage or knee brace is adequate for 2-4 weeks. The bandage can be removed when the patient experiences no pain at weight bearing. Early initiation of rehabilitation is recommended for improved outcomes. In the case of a grade II ligament injury, an above-knee cast or knee immobilizer is required for 3-6 weeks, depending on clinical examination findings during each review. Subsequently, it is replaced with a simple bandage or knee orthosis for a period of 2-4 weeks.

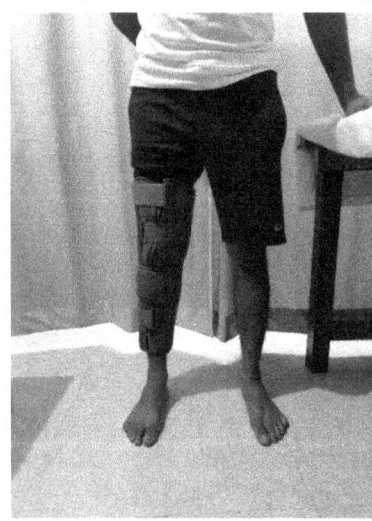

knee immobilizer

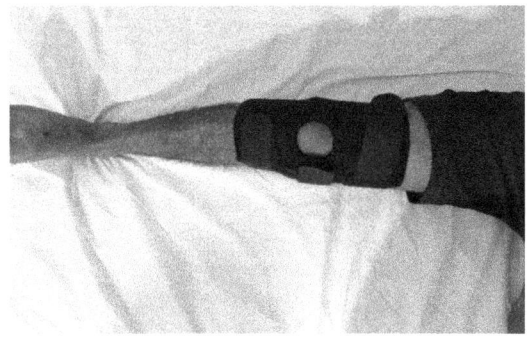
knee brace

POSTERIOR CRUCIATE LIGAMENT (PCL) TEAR

The most common cause of PCL tear (posterior cruciate ligament) is dashboard injury. If the dashboard injury is of high energy trauma, then there is a chance of posterior dislocation of the hip associated with the shaft of femur fracture. But if it's a minor injury there is a chance of Posterior cruciate ligament tear.

Ask the patient to flex the knee up to 90°. With this itself, it's possible to diagnose Posterior Cruciate Ligament tears. The phenomenon is called the **drop back phenomenon**.

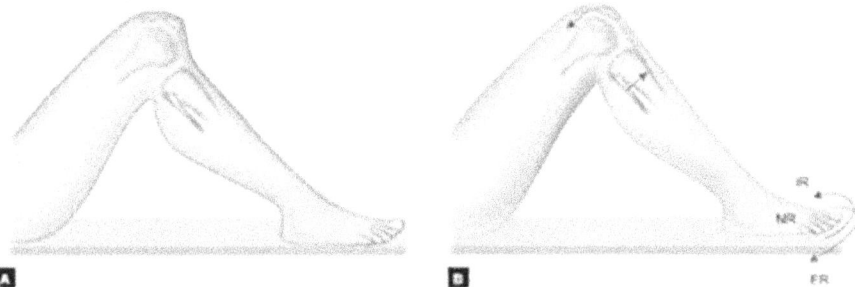

Drop-Back Phenomenon in PCL Tear

- In a normal knee joint at 90° flexion, the anterior cortex of the proximal tibia is 10 mm anterior to the distal femoral condyles.

- In a PCL tear, the patella appears more prominent, and the tibial tubercle is less prominent due to posterior subluxation of the tibia.

- The drop-back phenomenon, where the tibia drops posteriorly, is characteristic of PCL tears.

Godfrey's test

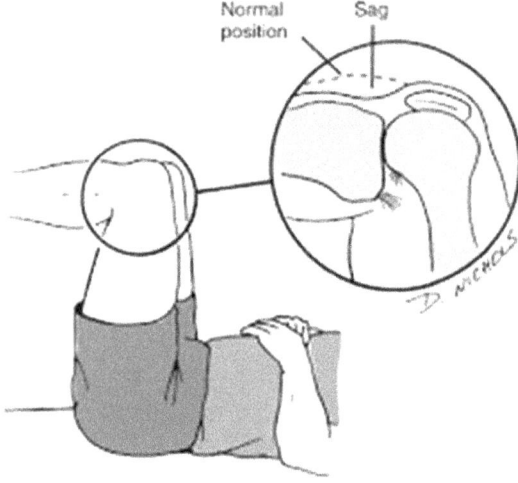

Position:
- Patient in the supine position.
- Hip and knee flexed to 90° (ninety-ninety position).

Observation:
- Assess for any posterior sag of the proximal tibia when compared to a normal knee joint.

Interpretation:
- A posterior sag indicates potential subluxation of the proximal tibia due to gravity, suggesting a Posterior Cruciate Ligament tear.

MENISCAL INJURY
- The reason for meniscal injury is sports injury mainly seen in young adults due to distinct strain applied to flexed and weight-bearing legs.
- Trap meniscus commonly splits longitudinally and its free edge may displace inwards towards the center of the joint which causes bucket handle tear. This prevents full

extension of the knee joint. Locking of the knee is a typical feature in bucket handle tears and whenever there is an attempt to straighten the knee, the painful elastic resistance is felt; which means springy blockage in extension. The last extension 20-30° is inhibited due to the bucket handle tear. If there is a bucket handle tear it requires surgical correction

- Giving way may be present in almost all meniscal injury
- Swelling will be associated with the condition but it may take time to swell when compared to anterior cruciate ligament tear.

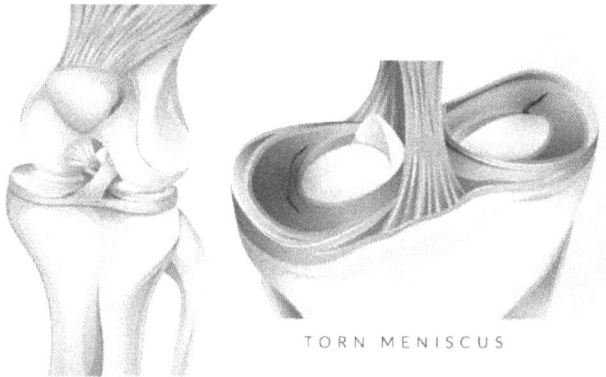

TORN MENISCUS

Applied anatomy

The meniscus is a C-shaped structure. It is triangular in cross-section. Only in the periphery of the meniscus, it is vascularised. The central part of the meniscus is avascular. The concave surface of the meniscus is loosely attached. The anterior horn is also loosely attached and the posterior horn is firmly attached. The medial meniscus is more prone to injury.

Clinical examination

<u>**1. Thessaly test**</u>

Position:

- Patient in the standing position.
- Examiner supports the patient's arm for balance.

Procedure:

- Patient stands on one leg (first on the normal side for comparison).
- Flexion of the knee to a maximum of 20°.
- Twisting of the femur on the tibia is performed.
- The procedure is repeated three times.

Interpretation:

- A positive test is indicated by pain over the joint line or a sensation of catching or locking during the maneuver.

2 Apley's grinding test

Position:

- Patient in prone position.

Procedure:

- Examiner flexes the knee to 90°.
- Examiner stabilizes the patient's thigh to the examination table.
- Compressive axial load is applied to the foot.
- Simultaneous rotation of foot is performed (either external or internal).

Interpretation:

- Pain or discomfort during compression and rotation may indicate meniscal pathology.
- Foot externally rotated is tested for medial meniscus and vice versa.

Reason for meniscal injury:

*Solely weight-bearing limb

*Flexion of that particular limb

* Distinct force applied i.e. twisting of the femur on the tibia.

KNEE COLLATERAL LIGAMENT INJURY

Out of both collateral ligaments of the knee medial and lateral; the medial collateral ligament is more prone to injuries. MCL injury is due to a direct hit over the knee from the lateral side. Valgus strain is the reason for medial collateral ligament injury. If force is more, along with Medial Collateral Ligament, Anterior Cruciate Ligament tear also occurs. The cause for lateral collateral ligament injury is a force from the medial side i.e. varus strain. MCL injury is common and the site of the tear is proximal, over its femoral attachment. LCL injury is rare. Commonly, the site of tear is distal, over fibular attachment. There is a potential risk of common peroneal nerve injury associated with the injury of knee LCL, which may end in foot drop. This condition requires reference.

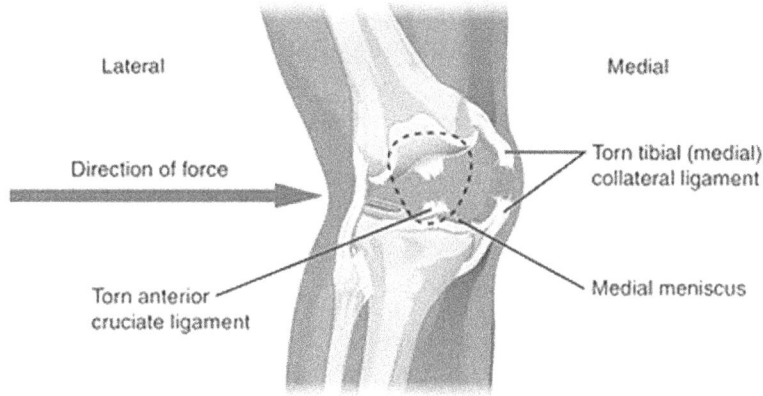

Anterior view

Clinical examination

- Abduction test (Valgus stress) for medial collateral ligament
- Adduction test (Varus stress) for lateral collateral ligament
- Apley's distraction test

Abduction or valgus stress test

Position:

- Patient is supine and the knee flexed to 30°.

Procedure:

- One hand acts as a fulcrum over the knee joint.
- The other hand applies abduction (valgus stress) to the knee.

Interpretation:

- Complete opening up of the knee joint over the medial side may indicate a complete tear or grade 3 tear of the medial collateral ligament (MCL), which requires surgical management.
- Partial tear may cause excruciating pain over the femoral attachment of the MCL.
- MCL tears are more prone to occur at the femoral attachment.

Additional Note:

- In complete knee extension, Abduction test can provide diagnosis of Anterior Cruciate Ligament (ACL) tear along with medial collateral ligament tear.

Apley's distraction test

Position:

- Patient in the prone position.

Procedure:
- Examiner's knee fixes the posterior thigh of the patient.
- Traction is applied to the foot, then internal and external rotation of foot is performed

Interpretation:
- Traction and external rotation may suggest a medial collateral ligament (MCL) injury.
- Traction and internal rotation may suggest a lateral collateral ligament (LCL) injury.

OTTAWA RULE OF KNEE[3]

- A knee X-ray series is only required for knee injury patients with any of these finding
  - Age >55 years
  - Isolated patellar tenderness without other bone tenderness
  - Tenderness of the fibular head.
  - Inability to flex the knee to 90°
  - Inability to bear weight immediately after injury and in the emergency department (4 steps) regardless of limping
- If all the above are negative, it's suggested to avoid prescription of X-ray.

NB. While eliciting tenderness it's suggested to check only at the patella. If the patellar tenderness is positive, ask the patient to do an active Straight leg raising and then it's advisable to take a radiological investigation.

Whenever there is a head of the fibula injury there is a chance of avulsion fracture due to the pull of the fibular collateral ligament or lateral collateral ligament of the knee joint. It causes injury to the common peroneal nerve and in turn causes foot drop. It's better to go for a radiological investigation and if needed, the patient should be referred.

KNEE JOINT PATHOLOGY
OSTEOARTHRITIS OF THE KNEE JOINT

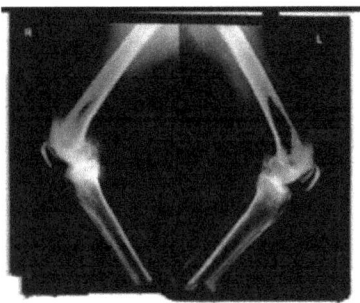 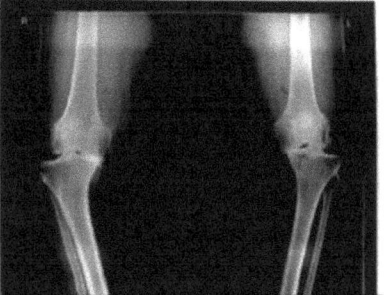

Grade IV OSTEOARTHRITIS WITH VARUS DEFORMITY

- It is considered a disease of old age (age group 45+).
- Pain worsens after exertion
- Swelling will be present and associated with pain
- The joint feels stiff after rest
- Pain is a feature of standing after a prolonged sitting.
- There will be pain when the patient gets up from bed. It's due to morning stiffness; which is a sign of inflammation associated with degeneration.
- It hurts the patient to get going because of morning stiffness.

Clinical features

*Age- disease of old age

*Sex – is almost equal

*Symptoms

1. Pain
2. Stiffness
3. Deformity
4. Swelling
5. Limping
6. Giving way

Physical signs

- Inspection- swelling and deformity
- Palpation- tenderness elicited mainly in the medial joint line, not warm, crepitus may be present
- Movement- as the disease progresses movement becomes more restricted.
- The range of motion of flexion is measured using a goniometer or the distance between the heel and buttocks is measured, on knee flexion.

Medial joint line

The medial joint line is palpated in a 90° flexed knee joint which is just medial to the patellar tendon. The patellar tendon connects the patella and tibial tuberosity. In a 90° flexed knee joint, it's possible to feel a hollow space between the medial femoral condyle and medial tibial condyle just medial to the patellar tendon.

In osteoarthritis patients the first point of tenderness is the medial joint line. These patients have vastus medialis obliquus (VMO) tenderness same as that of the medial joint line.

Pathologic changes with osteoarthritis

- Cartilage fragments are degenerated.
- Presence of cyst
- Osteophytes or bone spurs will be present
- Narrowing of joint space mainly the medial compartment
- Erosion of cartilage or bone

Grading of osteoarthritis, KL SCALE[4] (Kellgren and Lawrence system)

- **Grade 0** (none): definite absence of x-ray changes of osteoarthritis
- **Grade 1** : doubtful narrowing of joint space and possible osteophytic lipping
- **Grade 2** :definite osteophytes and possible narrowing of joint space; mainly medial compartment. Medial compartment will be lesser than the lateral compartment
- **Grade 3:** Moderate multiple osteophytes, definite narrowing of joint space, some sclerosis, and possible deformity of bone ends.
- **Grade 4** :Large osteophytes, marked narrowing of joint space, severe sclerosis, and definite deformity of bone ends

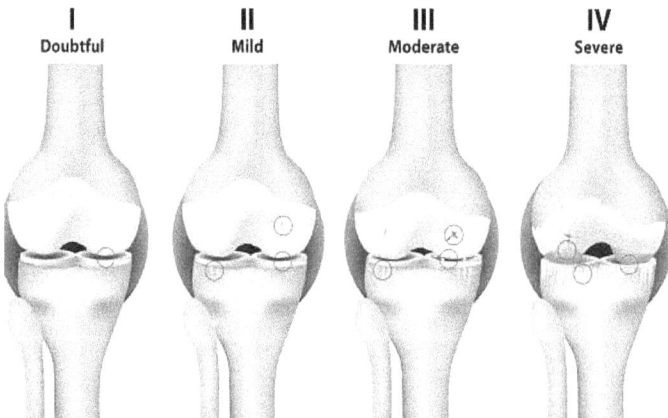

STAGE OF KNEE OSTEOARTHRITIS

I Doubtful   II Mild   III Moderate   IV Severe

Note: When patient's demand is high in grade 4, it is better to refer for surgical management i.e. Total Knee Replacement (TKR). And when demand is less, it is possible to try with conservative management and proper rehabilitation to maintain the quality of life. It's always advisable to take an X-ray of weight bearing (standing) AP view for KL scale grading of OSTEOARTHRITIS of knee.

Radiographic features

- Narrowing of joint space, usually asymmetrical
- Subchondral sclerosis
- Subchondral cysts
- Osteophyte formation
- Lack of osteoporosis

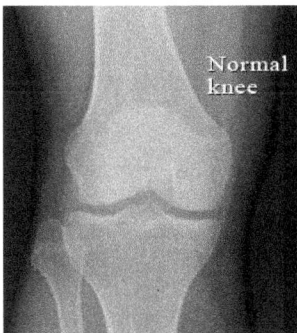
Figure 1

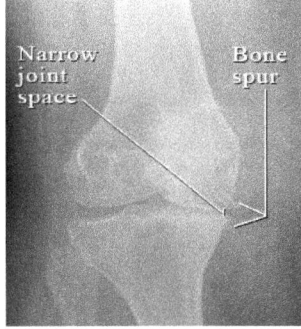
Figure 2

Note:

Always take AP view weight bearing or standing in Osteoarthritis patients for KL grading, otherwise, grade IV seems like grade II. In the picture given below, the top one is non-weight bearing and the below one is the weight bearing view of the same patient taken on the same day.

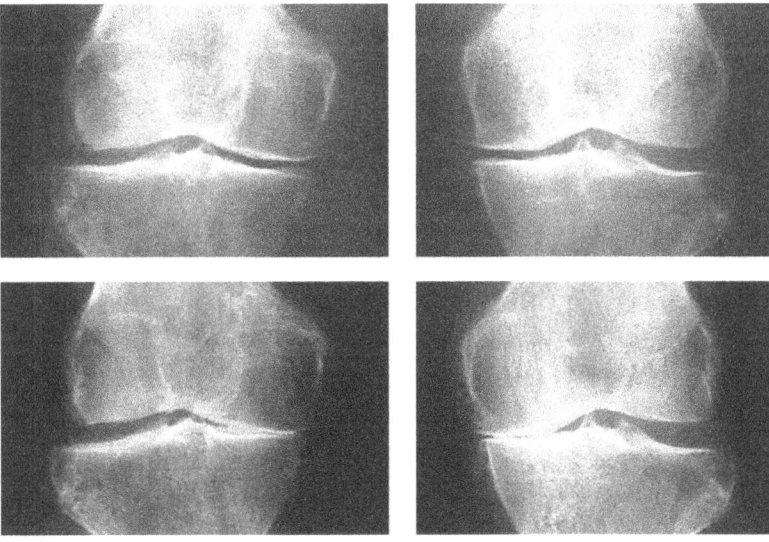

TIMED UP AND GO TEST (TUG TEST)

The Timed Up and Go test involves a patient walking from a seated position, covering a distance of 3 meters, turning back, and returning to the chair, followed by sitting down. A normal completion time is below 10 seconds. However, individuals with grade 3 osteoarthritis may take more than 30 seconds, experiencing pain at the start, during the turn, and while sitting. It is recommended to include this test in documentation for result review. Therefore, it should be conducted both at the beginning and end of the management to facilitate result comparison.

Management

- Initially ama pachana (follow general protocol explained under pathology)
- After ama pachana, it's advisable to change to transition phase
- Then internal sneha prayoga with a dose of 10ml and 20 ml as per the Agni (taila is better than ghrita) for about 14-21 days
- Rehabilitation after ama pachana
- Rasayana (to avoid recurrence)
- Nutritional consideration

Note:

Advise the patient to refrain from using orthosis beyond the acute phase. Prolonged use without concurrent rehabilitation may lead to quadriceps muscle wasting. In the case of grade IV OA, a knee brace is recommended for weight-bearing purposes. Continued rehabilitation alongside the use of the knee brace does not pose any harm.

Rehabilitation

The quadriceps should be given more strengthening along with the hamstring and the gastrocnemius.

Quadset:

Ask the patient to keep the pillow or a dress that is folded round in shape as a bandage just beneath the popliteal fossa. Ask the patient to compress that pillow or cloth downwards i.e. complete extension of the knee joint in which quadriceps will be tight holding for a period of 5 seconds and repeat it for 25 times.

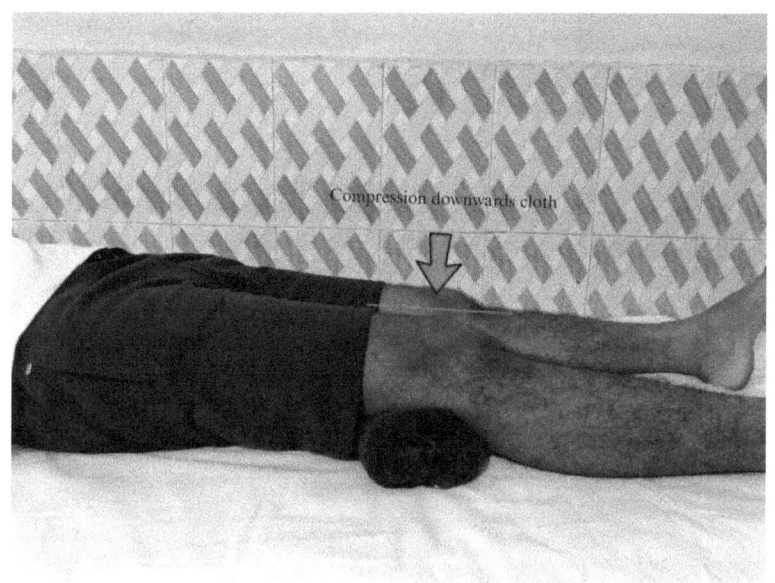

Note:

After ama pachana this exercise is to be advised and started, otherwise there will be aggravation of pain and symptoms.

Another variety of quad set in which a pillow or cloth is placed under the ankle joint followed by the above method

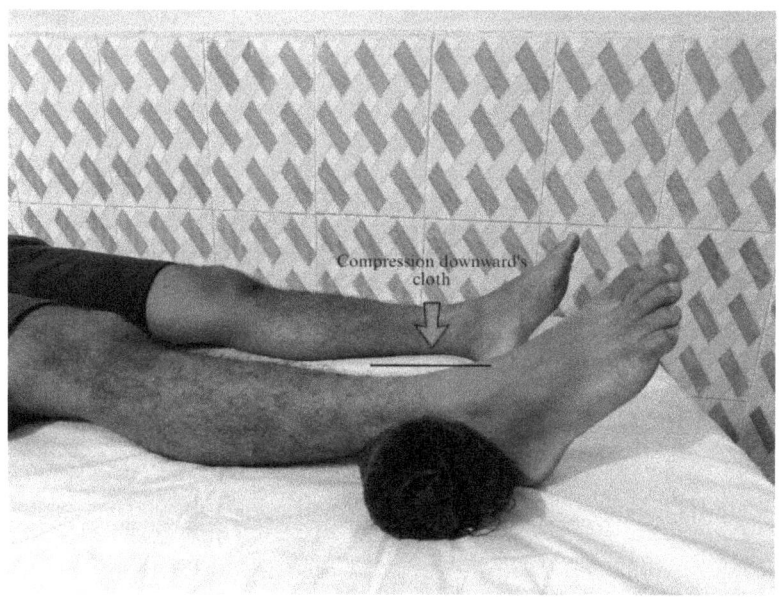

Pillow squeeze:

In this, a pillow is placed between both knees and the patient should squeeze the pillow. It should be done in a sitting posture or supine position. Hold it for 5 seconds and repeat it for 10 times

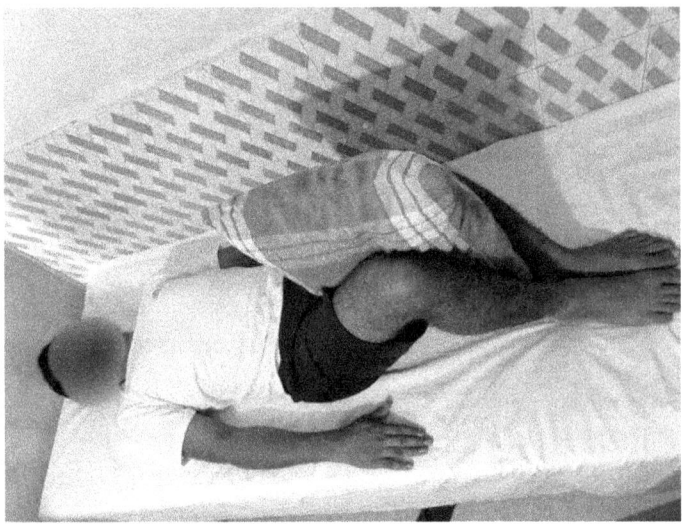

The next phase is **mobilization.**

SLR *(straight leg raising):*

This exercise is for the quadriceps and hamstring

Ask the patient to dorsiflex the foot and do the Straight Leg Raising. Along with quadriceps strengthening, it gives stretching to calf muscles. Hold it for 5 seconds and repeat it 10 times.

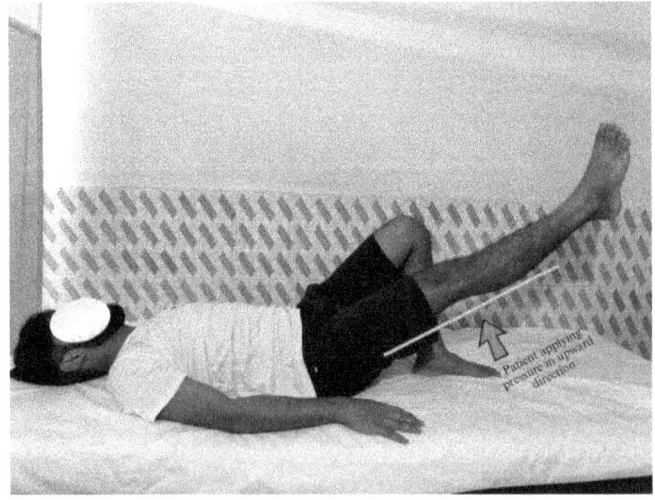

Ananthasana:

Also called a side leg lift. In the lateral position, advise the patient to raise the leg. The leg should be raised for 45° and hold it for 5 seconds and repeat it for 10 times.

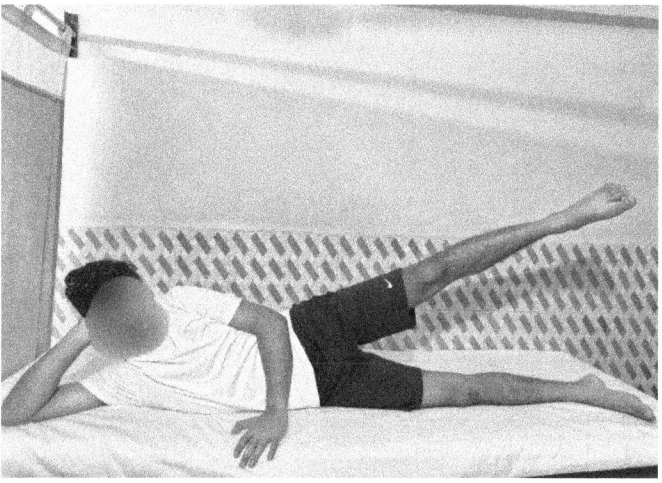

Chair march:

While in a sitting posture, instruct the patient to extend the knee, holding it for 5 seconds and repeating the process 10 times. It is advisable to dorsiflex the foot during this exercise for calf muscle stretching and quadriceps muscle strengthening. For individuals above 60 years old, recommend supporting the posterior thigh with both hands just above the knee to minimize discomfort during the exercise

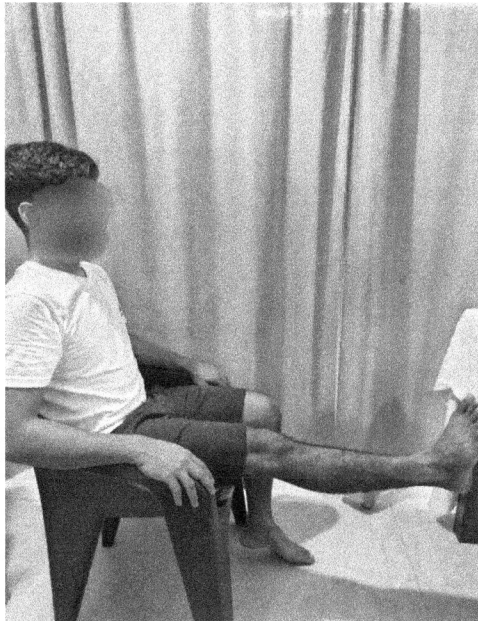

Weight bearing rehabilitation is advised at the last phase.

- **Toe raise**

Ask the patient to stand on their heel, no need to hold and it is repeated 10 times

- **Calf stretch**

In calf stretch the affected leg is placed on the posterior side and then the calf is stretched. Hold for 5 seconds and advice to repeat 10 times.

- **Stand on one leg**

This exercise is helpful at the last phase . A 10 sec stand, repeated for 10 times is good. To improve the proprioception and balance, it's better to do this exercise as eyes closed after 1 week.

Toe raise   calf stretch

Knee joint phase 1 rehabilitation

Knee joint phase 2 rehabilitation

Knee joint phase 3 rehabilitation

Difference in radiographic features of OSTEOARTHRITIS and RHEUMATOID ARTHRITIS

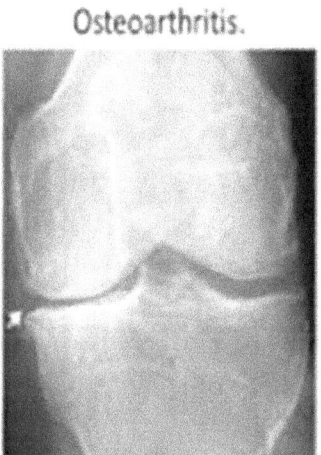
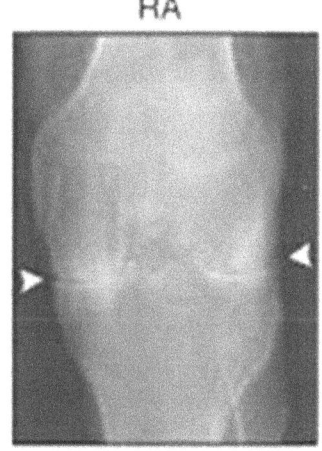

OSTEOARTHRITIS	RHEUMATOID ARTHRITIS
joint space reduction is asymmetrical	joint space reduction is symmetrical
osteophyte formation	osteophyte formation will be absent
Varus deformity more commonly	Valgus deformity more commonly
Osteoporosis will be absent	Osteoporosis present

- In Osteoarthritis joint space reduction is asymmetrical while in Rheumatoid arthritis it's symmetrical.
- In Osteoarthritis there will be osteophyte formation which will be absent in Rheumatoid arthritis
- In Osteoarthritis there is absence of osteoporosis but will be present in Rheumatoid arthritis
- In OSTEOARTHRITIS deformity more will be varus and in RHEUMATOID ARTHRITIS deformity is valgus commonly

OSGOOD SCHLATTER DISEASE(OSG)

Clinical presentation

A male patient in the age group between 14-16 presents with swollen and painful tibial tuberosity. It aggravates on exertion (runs, climbing stairs)

The most common point of tenderness is the tibial tuberosity to which the patellar tendon is attached.

Clinical examination

Extension of the knee against resistance will be painful at tibial tuberosity.

X-ray: lateral view – irregular fragmentation of apophysis to which ligament is attached

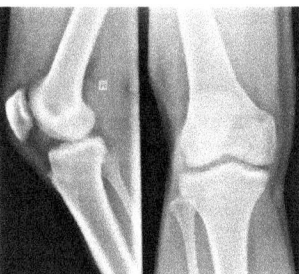

How to differentiate from Sinding-Larsen-Johansson syndrome

1. Age group 10-14
2. In this condition, the patellar tendon pulls the patella's lower pole, and this is Johanson Larsen syndrome.
3. Pain at the lower pole of the patella

4. On the extension of the knee against resistance, the patient feels pain at the lower pole of the patella

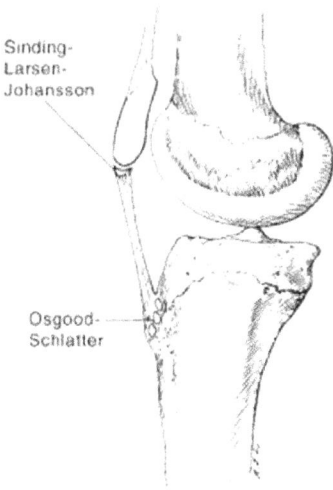

How to differentiate from patellar tendonitis

1. In the age group 16-30
2. Cause: repeated strain injury
3. On extension of the knee against resistance the patient felt pain over the patellar tendon

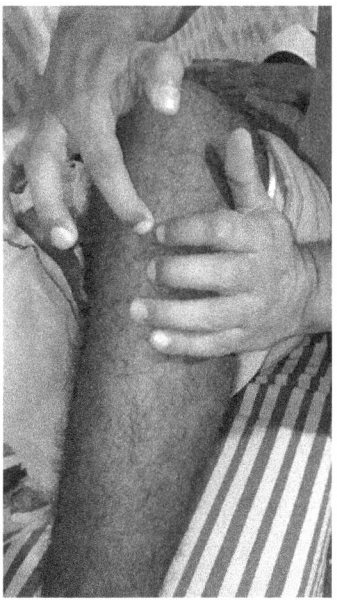

Management

- Ama pachana and sopha hara treatment (initial stage)
- In the later stage Internal sneha prayoga

- Pain management with bandage, orthosis, or lepa
- Rehabilitation (strengthening of quadriceps and patellar tendon)
- Proper hydration
- Proper nutritional supplements

Note:

Patients who need to play sports with pain can wear a patellar strap for the same during activities.

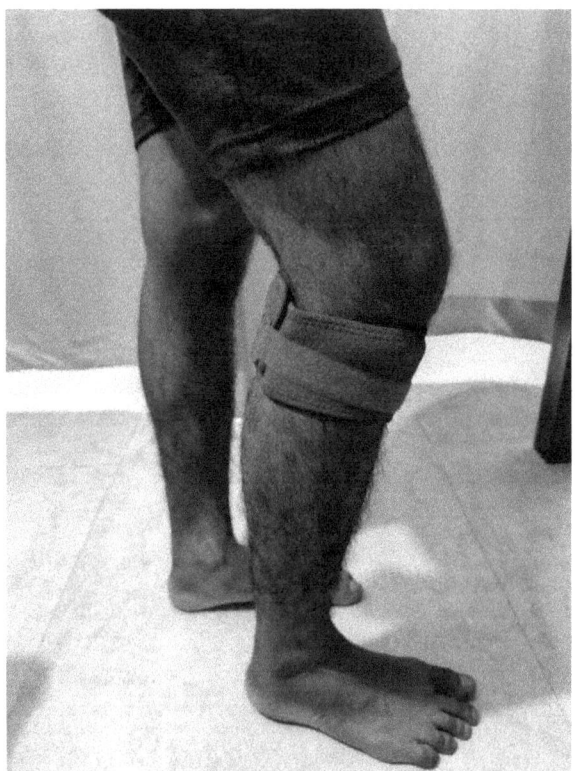

OSTEOCHONDRITIS DISSECANS(OCD)

Clinical presentation:

A male patient between the ages of 15 and 18 came to OPD with aching pain of knee and recurrent effusion.

The Osteochondritis Dissecans occur due to continuous impingement of the medial femoral condyle in between the tibial spine and cruciate ligament. A piece of bone becomes avascular and there will be demarcation between unhealthy bone and healthy bone. The most common site is the lateral part of the medial femoral condyle very close to the intercondylar notch.

Initially, there won't be locking. But in a later phase when this piece of bone becomes a loose body then there will be locking (means absence of final 30° extension). The final extension is arrested due to the loose body. Locking may also occur in meniscal tears, mainly bucket handle tears.

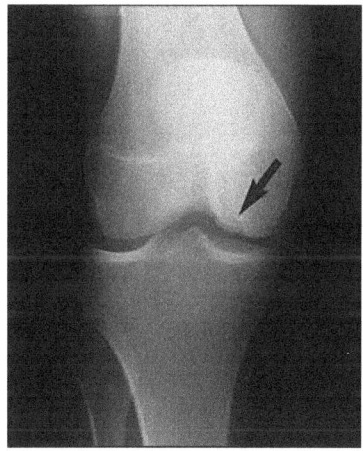 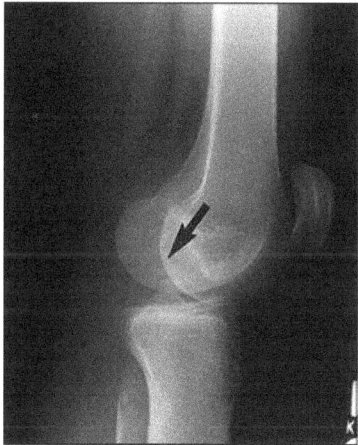

Clinical examination- Wilson's Test

Position:

- Patient in a sitting or supine posture.

Procedure:

- Complete flexion of the knee.
- Passive internal rotation of the foot by the examiner.
- Then Extension of the knee.

Interpretation:

- Pain over the medial femoral condyle during knee extension and internal rotation of the foot.
- Pain subsides when the foot is returned to a neutral position.

Treatment protocol

- In the initial phase laksha, madhuka, and lasuna 10 GM each as ksheera kashaya is useful.
- Advise quadriceps strengthening rehab and other exercises with proper weight-bearing. Weight-bearing improves circulation.
- If there is loose body, it needs to be excised when locking is present

ILIOTIBIAL BAND SYNDROME (ITBS)

Clinical presentation:

- Pain over the lateral femoral condyle
- In the age group 15-25
- History of repeated running, repeated cycling.
- Another clinical presentation is 50 years male or female those who walk slanting surfaces holding weight in hand.

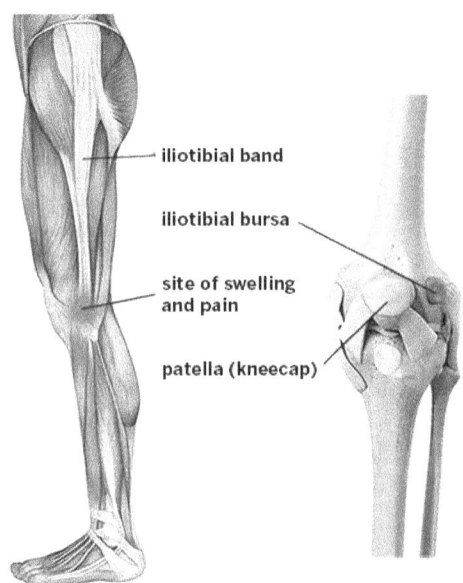

- It is a Repeated Strain Injury
- The iliotibial band runs along the lateral thigh in between the Tensor fascia Lata and Gluteus Maximus and attaches to the lateral tibial condyle.
- The point of friction on repeated flexion and extension of the knee joint is over the lateral femoral condyle, 2 cm proximal to the lateral joint line

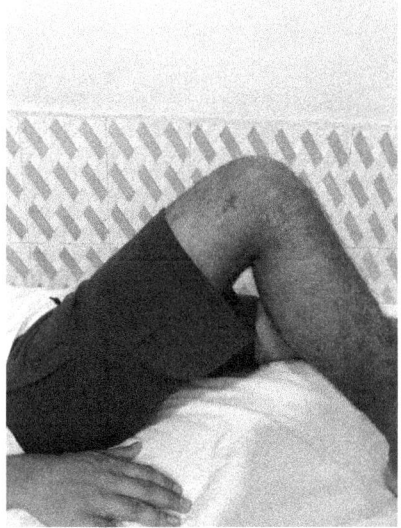

Site of ITBS

Clinical examination:

Renne's test

Ask the patient to stand on the affected leg and flex the knee up to 30°. Up to flexion of 30° itself, the patient felt pain over the lateral femoral condyle

Noble test

Hold the lateral femoral condyle with the examiner's thumb. Ask the patient for repeated flexion and extension of the knee joint which causes pain over the iliotibial band.

The Ilio tibial support is found to be effective during activities in iliotibial band syndrome in the beginning phase, if the patient wants to continue sports activities.

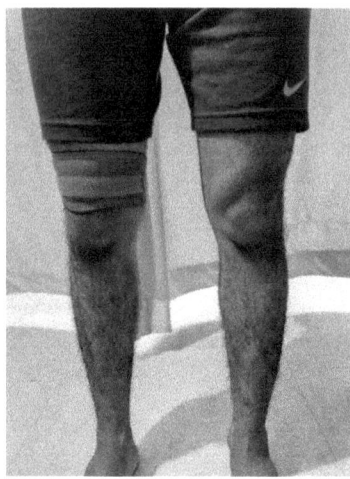

Note:

Continuous use of a Ilio tibial support should not be encouraged.

Modified Srunga/Alabu

It's possible to perform modified Srunga/Alabu in the most tender point. Suction is made after eliciting tenderness. Then do pricking with the No. 12 blade attached to the BP handle or a No. 18 needle and continue the suction. 2- 2.5 ml of blood is taken out by this procedure. The patient feels immediate relief after this procedure. It's better to start rehabilitation on the next day.

Agnikarma

The area should be cleaned and made shalaka heated to red-hot. It's recommended to use a blow torch to make shalaka red hot. Agnikarma is done at the most tender point, i.e. 2 cm proximal to the lateral joint line. It should be done in 6-9 spots. Ruksha agnikarma is done. After Agni karma, a simple bandage for one day is advisable.

Ayurvedic management

- Initially ama pachana is done
- Raktamoksha and Agnikarma, based on condition (not needed in every case).
  - If there is pitta prakopa, modified Srunga / Alabu is recommended and if there is no pitta kopa, agnikarma is suggested.

- o Upanaha can be done with nagaradi or ellumnishadi choorna, prior to Agnikarma.
- Internal sneha prayoga and Rasayana to avoid recurrence

Note:

Anusastra shall be incorporated in sports persons who need quick recovery and return to sports with early rehabilitation. In other patients, if conservative management fails for 3-4 weeks, it's advisable to do anusastra as per the condition of the patient.

CHONDROMALACIA PATELLA

Clinical presentation:

- Pain over retro patellar area or anterior knee pain
- Most commonly females are affected
- Typically in ages 30-40
- In sportsperson pain may start in second decade
- The condition aggravates whenever the patient stands after sitting for a prolonged time or walks on slopes or climbing down stairs i.e. when the knee comes to complete extension while stepping down patients feel typical pain

Clarke's test

Position:

- Patient in supine position.

Procedure:

- Fix the superior margin of the affected patella with the examiner's web space of the thumb and index finger.
- Ask the patient to contract the quadriceps or press the knee downwards.

Interpretation:

- On quadriceps contraction, patella moves proximally, which is resisted by examiner's web space, producimg retro patellar pain. This provides a confirmed diagnosis.

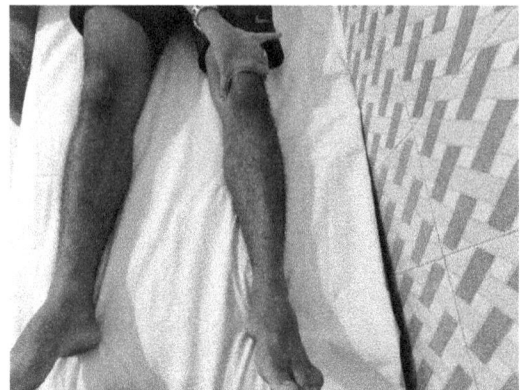

Facet tenderness test

The patient should lie in a supine position and the knee should be in complete extension. Elevate the medial margin of the patella and palpate the medial facet. This test will be positive in chondromalacia patella.

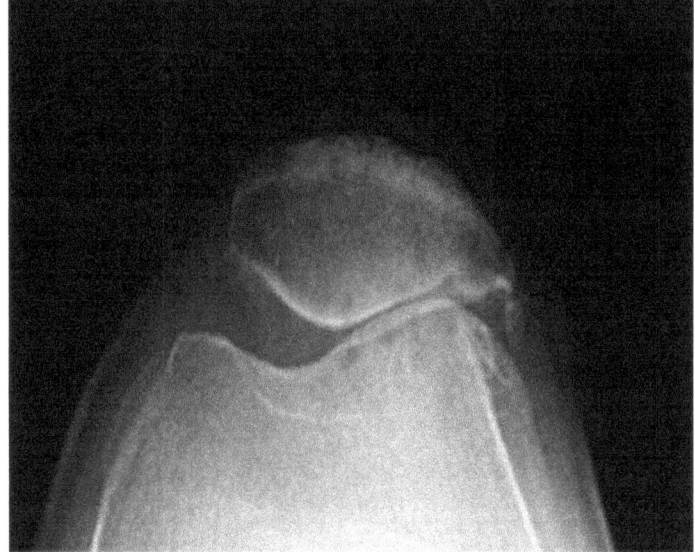

Cartilage in between the patella and femur is affected.

Xray- normal skyline view

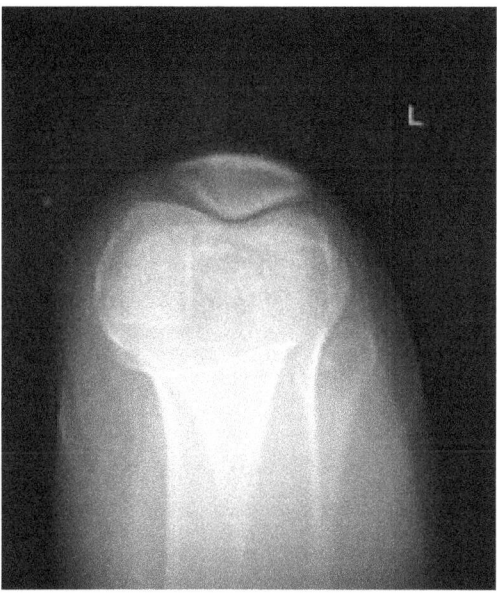

Insall Salvati Index (Assessed in knee lateral view X-ray)

1. is the distance between the lower pole of patella and the tibial tubercle
2. is the distance between the lower pole and upper pole of the patella

Insall Salvati Index (ISI) =1/2

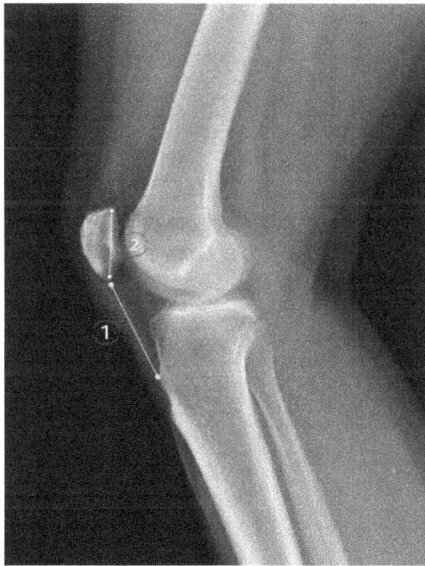

The normal value of insall-salvati index is calculated by one divided by two and it must be between 0.8- 1.2

- When Insall Salvati differs it may be due to patella alta or patella Baja.

- In patella alta, Insall salvati index is >1.2. In such cases, there will be instability of the patella.

o In the case of patella alta, there is an increased risk of chondromalacia patella and recurrent patellar dislocation.

Rehabilitation for chondromalacia patella

- Pelvic lift
- pillow squeeze
- salabhasana

Management

- Initial stage is ama pachana and sophahara, since there is inflammation
- Rehabilitation along with internal sneha prayoga

Questions for self practice

1. Clinical examination test for meniscal tear
2. Complication of fibular collateral ligament tear
3. ACL tear caused by which type of injury
4. Clinical examination of chondromalacia patella
5. Grading of OA knee
6. Reduction method of lateral dislocation of patella

CASE PRESENTATION – PATELLAR SUBLUXATION

A female patient aged 24 years presented in a wheelchair to op, with severe pain of right knee, with a history of injury.

History

- The pain initiated after a twisting injury to the knee, when the patient swiftly transitioned from a standing position to sitting, involving a sudden movement of knee flexion from extension.

Attitude

- Flexed knee, unable to extend affected knee

Clinical features
- Severe pain, deformity and unable to attempt any movements
- A swelling over lateral femoral condyle

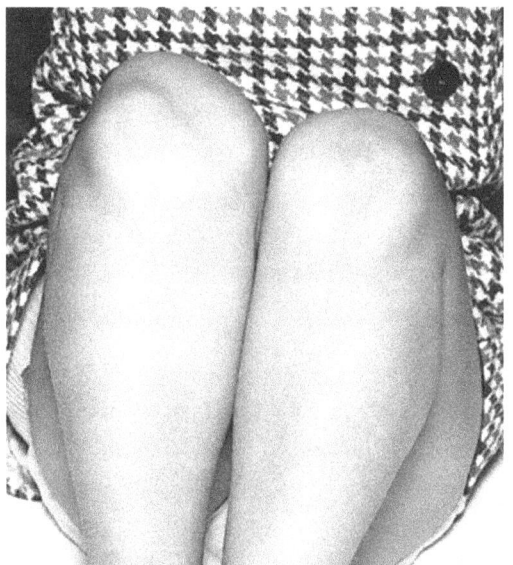

Radiological investigation
- X-ray- skyline view of patella

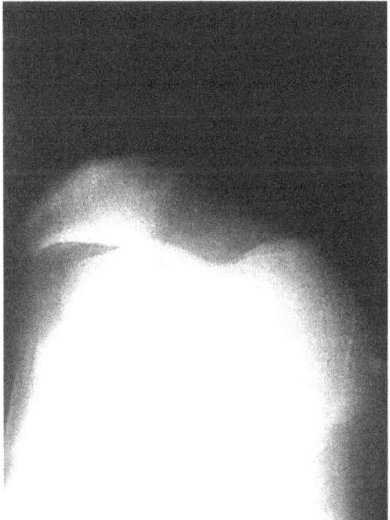

Diagnosis
- Lateral dislocation of patella (Always lateral)

Management
- Reduction is by giving firm pressure over the patella medially as displacement is lateral
- Simultaneously the leg is extended which provides reduction and relief for pain.
- A knee immobilizer or posterior cast bandage for three weeks is a must for the healing of soft tissue. There may be a chance of an MPFL (medial patellofemoral ligament) sprain.
- After the removal of bandage, rehab is a must to avoid recurrence.

As per Acharya Surutha, the method of reduction of janu should be followed the same as that of koorpara i.e. angushtena anumarjanam, prasarana and aakunchanam.

NB. Prognosis of recurrent dislocation of patella due to structural defects such as increased Q angle, patella alta and trochlear dysplasia are not much good. In such cases with structural or anatomical variants, if there is no relief in 8 weeks of rehab and conservative management, take a second opinion from an orthopedic surgeon.

SUMMARY OF KNEE INJURY AND PATHOLOGY

Absolutely, a clear and accurate diagnosis is crucial for the effective management of knee joint conditions. The knee joint is susceptible to various injuries, including ligament sprains, meniscus tears, and patellar dislocations, as well as degenerative conditions such as osteoarthritis. While some rare situations may require surgical intervention, many knee issues can indeed respond well to conservative management.

Internal medications for ama pachana and sopha hara, play a role in managing symptoms, but a comprehensive approach often involves internal sneha, rehabilitation and rasayana. Focusing on specific muscle groups, including the vastus medialis obliquus (VMO), is a key component of rehabilitation for knee issues.

The VMO is part of the quadriceps muscle group and plays a crucial role in stabilizing the patella during movement. Weakness or imbalance in the quadriceps, particularly the VMO, can contribute to patellar instability and may exacerbate certain knee conditions.

Rehabilitation exercises targeting the VMO, along with overall quadriceps strengthening and flexibility exercises, can help improve joint stability and function.

When a patient comes to op with a monoarticular knee joint pain, please keep these things in mind while assessing the case.

Differential diagnosis of monoarticular joint pain

1. Congenital - congenital bipartite patella
2. Trauma - any injury
3. Neoplasia - osteosarcoma
4. Inflammatory - rheumatoid arthritis (better to adopt modified ACR/EULAR criteria for diagnosis), reactive arthritis (classic triad of urethritis, conjunctivitis, arthritis)

5. Biochemical - Gout
6. Endocrine - diabetic charcot
7. Degenerative - Osteoarthritis
8. Vascular- hemophilia hemarthrosis
9. Psychogenic
10. Infection - septic arthritis.

NB. Knee is the most common joint affected with Septic arthritis. Kocher's criteria shall be considered for the diagnosis of Septic arthritis.

- Non weight bearing
- fever higher than 101.3°F
- ESR above 40 mm/hour
- white blood cell count greater than 12,000 cells/mm^3

If all four are positive, then the chance of septic arthritis may be above 98 %. If all four are negative, then the chance of septic arthritis may be below 0.2 %. Never miss the diagnosis. Immediate reference to an orthopedic surgeon is inevitable in this situation.

INJURY MANAGEMENT KNEE

Approach to the management of acute injuries aligns with standard practice, particularly in situations where immediate immobilization is required due to severe pain and the inability to conduct detailed special examinations. The initial focus on history, inspection, and palpation allows for a provisional diagnosis and the initiation of appropriate interventions to address pain and inflammation.

On the second or third visit, after pain relief, it's better to do special examinations and make a precise diagnosis. If there is a suspicion of complete tear, it's advisable to take an MRI in between a period of 3 to 6 weeks after injury. In cases where a complete tear is suspected, obtaining a confirmed diagnosis through more advanced imaging, such as MRI, is a prudent step.

In a grade I injury, it's possible to remove bandage by 2-4 weeks and start rehab in full swing. Grade II injury may take around 6-10 weeks for pain relief and to remove bandage. The phased approach to rehabilitation, with gradual progression based on the severity of the injury (Grade I, Grade II), is in line with the principles of allowing sufficient time for healing and minimizing the risk of re-injury. Starting rehabilitation after pain relief and when the tissue has undergone initial healing is crucial for promoting optimal recovery.

Overall, our approach emphasizes the importance of a thorough and evolving diagnostic process, personalized treatment plans, and a gradual return to activity based on the specific needs of each patient and the nature of their injury.

What's the advice to a complete ACL tear who came for a second opinion regarding surgery ?

Advice for managing a complete ACL tear takes into account both the patient's level of activity and their specific demands, providing a thoughtful approach based on individual circumstances.

Sports person with High Demand:

- For individuals highly active in sports, particularly where stability is crucial, recommend definitive management through surgery. This aligns with common practices, as surgical intervention is often preferred for athletes who need to regain optimal knee stability for competitive sports.

Non-Sports Person or Low Demand:

- For patients with lower activity demands or those who may not engage in high-impact sports, propose a trial of conservative management.
- Conservative management includes internal medicine management protocol with a focused rehabilitation program lasting 6-8 weeks, emphasizing strength, flexibility, and proprioception exercises.

Assessment of Stability:

- After the conservative management phase, it's a must to assess the stability of the knee.
- This assessment involves activities such as walking fast and making swift changes in direction, replicating scenarios that might challenge the knee's stability.

Decision Point:

- If, during these activities, the affected knee gives way or exhibits instability, it's better to consider surgical correction. This indicates that the knee may not have achieved sufficient stability through conservative measures alone.

Continued Rehabilitation:

- If the knee remains stable during these assessments, the patient is advised to continue with regular rehabilitation. This involves ongoing exercises and activities to maintain and enhance knee function.

This approach reflects the consideration of the patient's lifestyle, activity level, and individual goals in making decisions about whether to pursue surgery. It highlights the importance of tailoring the treatment plan to the specific needs of each patient, recognizing that not all individuals may require immediate surgical intervention, especially if they can achieve satisfactory function and stability through rehabilitation.

PATHOLOGY MANAGEMENT KNEE

Clinical Diagnosis:

- Pathological situations involving the knee demand a precise diagnosis.
- In most cases, it's possible to diagnose knee conditions through a thorough examination.

Differential Diagnosis:

- Conditions like iliotibial band syndrome (ITBS) and patellar tendonitis, patients complain of knee pain.
- Consider the differential diagnosis involving the spine, hip, and knee is critical.

Impact on Prognosis and Prescription:

- Recognizing the differential diagnosis is not only essential for accurate diagnosis but also influences the assessment of prognosis, prescription, and rehabilitation.

Individualized Approaches:

- Stressing the importance of customization in approaches based on factors such as the affected structure, age, and sex of the patient indicates a patient-centered and personalized strategy.

Caution Against Prescribing Without Assessment:

- The warning against prescribing without clinical assessment underscores the significance of avoiding one-size-fits-all approaches and emphasizes the need for individualized care.

What's the advice to a grade IV OA patient regarding total knee replacement (TKR) ?

Considering both clinical and radiological assessments, understanding the patient's demands regarding routine activities, and incorporating validated outcome measures should be incorporated for a comprehensive and patient-centered strategy.

Clinical and radiological assessments:

This approach recognizes the importance of not solely relying on imaging but also considering the patient's symptoms and functional status.

Patient Demand:

Understanding the patient's demands and lifestyle, such as the need to climb stairs, adds a practical dimension to prognosis. Understanding the patient's expectations and requirements is crucial for setting realistic treatment goals.

Prognostic Factors:

Like stability considerations in ACL complete tears, pain is a significant factor in this context. Pain, along with other prognostic factors, can guide decisions about the potential success of conservative management.

Conservative Management and Rehabilitation:

An 8-week trial of conservative management with proper rehabilitation

The emphasis on regular rehabilitation and ongoing assessment after the initial 8 weeks ensures a dynamic and adaptive approach to the patient's needs.

Outcome Measures:

The use of validated outcome measures such as WOMAC (Western Ontario and McMaster Universities Arthritis Index), KOOS (Knee injury and Osteoarthritis Outcome Score) and TUG (Timed Up and Go) Test demonstrates a commitment to evidence-based practice and objective assessment of the patient's progress.

Functional Improvement Criteria:

The criteria of achieving routine activities with 70-80% relief for pain after 8 weeks provide a clear benchmark for evaluating the success of conservative management. This approach combines both quantitative and qualitative assessments.

This approach integrates various facets of patient care, considering not only the clinical and radiological aspects but also the patient's lifestyle and functional needs. The use of standardized outcome measures adds objectivity to the assessment process, contributing to a well-rounded and patient-centric strategy.

NB. To ensure the appropriateness of recommendations regarding total knee replacement (TKR), **it is crucial to conduct thorough clinical and radiological assessments**. Additionally, understanding **the patient's specific demands** and their **commitment to regular rehabilitation** is essential. Blindly providing advice without considering these factors may not result in meaningful guidance**.**

The advice to patients with Baker's cyst

Baker's cyst is secondary to

Injury

- ACL, MENISCUS TEAR

Pathology

- OSTEOARTHRITIS, RHEUMATOID ARTHRITIS

Treatment for the primary disease is the management of Baker's cyst.

Quick assessment knee

- Thessaly test - meniscus tear
- TUG - assessment of OA
- Clarke's - chondromalacia patella
- Lachman - ACL tear
- Abduction test - MCL tear

- Renne's - ILIOTIBIAL BAND SYNDROME (ITBS)
- Locking of knee - bucket handle tear of meniscus

NB. **Knee buckling without pain** is not orthopaedic, its' **neurological**. The main causes are:

- Myopathy
- Femoral nerve palsy
- L3 root lesion
- Tumour in spinal canal
- Pedunculated tumour in 4th ventricle
- Cortical lesion

CLINICAL PEARLS- KNEE

EXAMINATION OF INJURY OF KNEE -nutshell

History

Mechanism

- Blow on the lateral side – medial collateral ligament injury
- Blow on the medial side – lateral collateral ligament injury
- Dashboard injury – posterior cruciate ligament tear
- Knee hyperextended – anterior cruciate ligament injury
- Femur internally rotated on tibia – medial meniscus injury
- Femur externally rotated on tibia – lateral meniscus injury

Locking of the knee means the joint can be flexed freely, but cannot extend beyond a certain degree.

1. **Inspection**

Two knees are completely exposed and placed in identical positions. Inspection should be made from all aspects including the popliteal fossa.

Attitude:

- Check if the knee is locked in a flexed position, abducted or adducted, hyperextended, or displaced backward.

Swelling:

- Ligament Injury: Serosanguinous effusion.
- Bony Injury: Hemorrhagic effusion.
- Note abnormal swelling over the lateral condyle of the femur, which can occur in dislocation of the patella.

Muscular Wasting:
- Observe for signs of muscular wasting, which may indicate an old injury.

2. Palpation

Elicit the exact point of tenderness.

- Tenderness at the femoral attachment of the medial collateral ligament suggests a tear of the medial collateral ligament.
- Tenderness at a joint level midway between the ligamentum patella and tibial collateral ligament suggests a torn anterior horn of the medial meniscus.
- Tenderness posterior to the tibial collateral ligament is diagnostic of a torn posterior horn of medial meniscus

2. Palpation of the patella – palpate patella as a whole. Ask to lift the extended leg. If possible, then the extensor apparatus of the knee is patent.
3. Palpation of the lower end of the femur – if any deformity, check the distal pulse. There is a chance of supracondylar fracture of femur, which may cause popliteal artery damage.
4. Palpation of the upper end of the tibia and fibula – lateral condyle of the tibia is more frequently fractured. Springing tests can be done. It may require CT 3D view for better understanding of displacement.

3. Measurements
- The breadth of the lower end of the femur and the upper end of the tibia
- Circumference of thigh and calf at fixed points from joint line to check muscular wasting.

4. Movements
- If the patient cannot extend the leg, there is injury to the extensor mechanism so please avoid flexion in that case.
- Absence of extension at final thirty degree is suggestive of bucket handle tear of meniscus or loose body.

5. Special tests
- **Thessaly's test** – test to detect medial and lateral meniscus tear.
- **Apley's Grinding test** – medial and lateral meniscus tear.
- **Apley's Distraction test** – medial and lateral collateral ligament tear.
- **Adduction and Abduction test** – medial and lateral collateral ligament tear.
- **Drawer sign** – anterior and posterior cruciate ligament tear.
- **Lachman test** – anterior and posterior cruciate ligament tear.

X-ray
- AP view - weight bearing/standing in OA knee, non weight bearing in injury
- Lateral view- non -weight bearing
- Skyline view - patellar dislocation, chondromalacia patella
- Tunnel view - osteochondritis dissecans
- Forced abduction and adduction – to rule out MCL and LCL injury

EXAMINATION OF PATHOLOGY OF KNEE -nutshell

A. **Inspection** - standing, sitting, supine, and prone position, both from front and back

Gait:
- Carefully observe the gait of the patient.

Attitude:
- Note any moderate flexion, genu valgum, or genu varus.
- Pay attention to the anterior surface and position of the patella if the knee is in a flexed position.

Swelling:
- Check for bilateral swelling.
- Identify swelling in specific areas:
- Prepatellar, infrapatellar, and suprapatellar swelling can indicate bursitis.
- Baker's cyst is associated with Osteoarthritis, Rheumatoid arthritis and Tuberculosis.

Muscular Wasting:
- Observe muscular wasting both above and below the knee.

B. Palpation

1. Local temperature and tenderness

2. Swelling – fluctuation and patellar tap

3. Popliteal fossa – in the prone position

4. Bony components – tenderness, irregularity, and swelling. Crepitus indicates Osteoarthritis

5. Patella – push patella medially and laterally, crepitus indicates chondromalacia patella

C. Movements

Both active and passive movements are noted

D. Measurements

Thigh measured to check wasting.

E. **Lymph node** – inguinal lymph node is palpated in knee arthritis.

Very important – check hip joint and upper lumbar spine tests, Femoral Nerve Stretch Test (FNST)

NB. In young patients aged 5 to 20 experiencing knee joint pain, it is imperative to recommend X-ray investigation. **Osteosarcoma** poses a potential risk in this age group, with a higher incidence in the distal femur and proximal tibia.

9. ANKLE JOINT

Applied Anatomy
- The ankle joint is formed by the tibia and fibula and the talus.
- Ankle Joint:
- The connection between the tibia, fibula, and talus, allowing for dorsiflexion and plantarflexion.
- Subtalar Joint:
- The joint between the talus and calcaneus, contributing to inversion and eversion movements.
- Midtarsal (Transverse Tarsal) Joint:
- Located between the hindfoot and midfoot, enabling side-to-side foot movements.

Ligaments:
- Various ligaments provide stability to the ankle joint, including the lateral ligaments (anterior talofibular, middle calcaneofibular, and posterior talofibular) and the medial (deltoid) ligament.
- The lateral ligaments are more commonly injured due to their relative weakness compared to the strong deltoid ligament on the medial side

Tendons:
- Tendons surrounding the ankle play a crucial role in movement. Notable tendons include the Achilles tendon and the anterior and posterior tibialis tendons.

Achilles Tendon:
- The Achilles tendon, which attaches the calf muscles to the calcaneus, is essential for plantarflexion.

Tarsal Bones:
- Seven tarsal bones form the hindfoot and midfoot, including the calcaneus, talus, navicular, cuboid, and the three cuneiform bones.
- The talus bone is a key player in ankle movement, articulating with the tibia and fibula.

Fascia and bursa :
- The plantar fascia is a thick band of connective tissue on the sole of the foot. It extends from the calcaneus to the toes and plays a crucial role in supporting the arches of the foot.

- Retrocalcaneal Bursa: Positioned between the Achilles tendon and the calcaneus, it minimizes friction during ankle movement. Inflammation of this bursa can lead to retrocalcaneal bursitis.

Movements:
- Dorsiflexion
- Plantar flexion
- Inversion
- Eversion

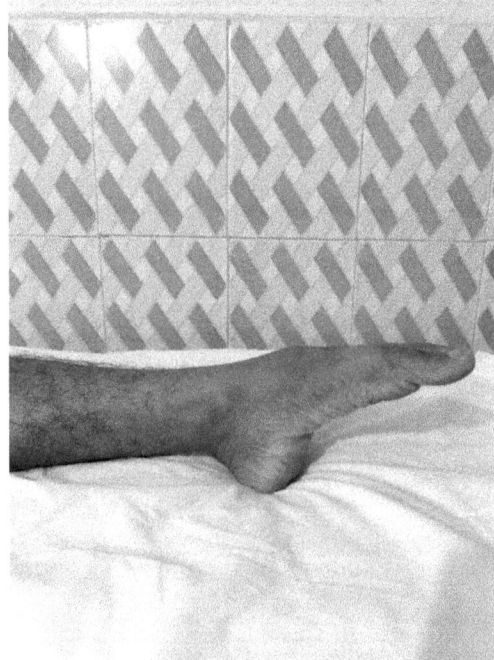
plantar flexion

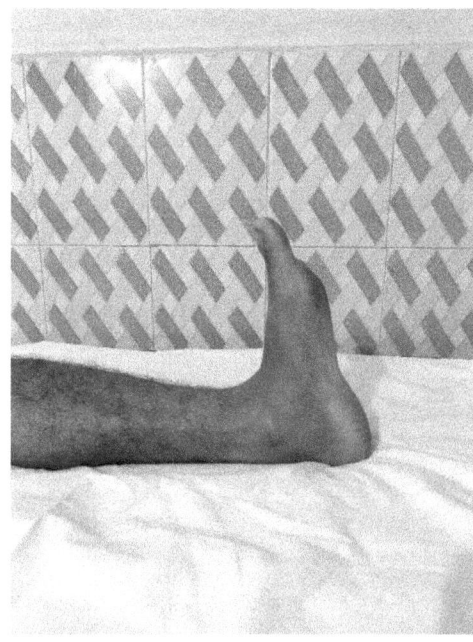 dorsiflexion

Range of Movement (ROM)

o Dorsiflexion – 15°

o Plantarflexion – 55°

Subtalar joint

o Eversion – 10°

o Inversion – 20°

Feet - subtalar + midtarsal + tarsometatarsal joint movements

o Supination – 35°

o Pronation – 20°

Metatarsophalangeal joint – the great toe

o Flexion – 40°

Interphalangeal joint – great toe

o Flexion – 60°

EXAMINATION OF INJURIES ANKLE JOINT

History is very important to know the mechanism of injury.

A. Inspection:

Deformity:

- Carefully observe for any deformities of the foot.

B. Palpation:

i. All bones of the ankle.

ii. Check for tenderness just below the lateral malleolus, which could suggest a lateral collateral ligament sprain.

iii. Perform springing to rule out distal end fractures.

iv. Palpate the tendo Achilles (Thompson test).

- The Thompson test involves squeezing the calf while the patient lies prone, and the absence of foot movement during the squeeze may indicate an Achilles tendon tear.

C. Movements:

- Assess slight active and passive movements of the foot.

D. **Measurements** –

Medial Malleolus to the Head of First Metatarsal:

- This measurement helps evaluate the longitudinal arch of the foot.

Medial Malleolus to the Point of the Heel:

- It involves measuring from the medial malleolus to the most posterior point of the heel.

Lateral Malleolus to the Head of Fifth Metatarsal:

- This measurement evaluates the lateral aspect of the foot.

Investigations

X-ray

Ankle joint

- AP view
- Lateral view
- Ankle mortise view (15-20° internal rotation of leg from AP view)
- Strained AP view – ligament tear conditions

Calcaneum

- Lateral view (to evaluate Tuber-joint angle or Bohler's angle)
- Axial view

Metatarsal

- Dorsal-plantar
- Oblique

Alignment in foot x-ray

- medial borders of 2nd metatarsal and intermediate cuneiform should line up on the DP (dorsoplantar) view of foot
- medial borders of 3rd metatarsal and lateral cuneiform should line up on the oblique view of foot

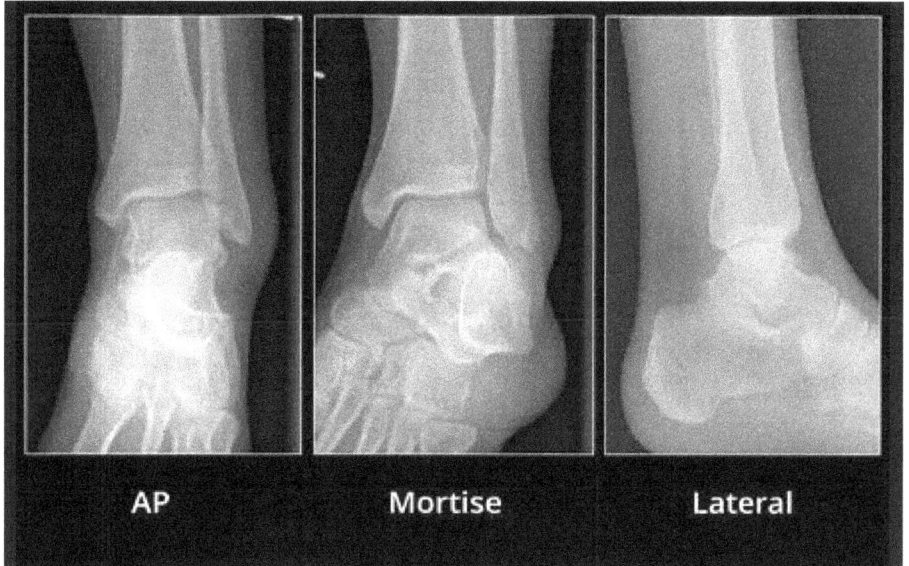

Differential diagnosis
- LCL Sprain
  - Tenderness Below lateral Malleolus
  - This could be indicative of ligamentous involvement, commonly the lateral collateral ligaments, mostly anterior talofibular ligament.
- Distal End Fibula Fracture:
  - The springing test involves squeezing the tibia and fibula to elicit pain. A positive springing test when squeezed on proximal tibia and fibula might indicate a fracture at the distal fibula. However, this should be confirmed with imaging studies.
- Distal End Tibia Fracture:
  - Inability to bear weight could be a sign of a significant lower leg injury, possibly a fracture. X-rays are essential to diagnose and assess the severity of the fracture. If there is avulsion of medial malleolus due to deltoid ligament, it requires surgical reference.
- Calcaneus Fracture Imaging:
  - Imaging, including axial view and Lateral view. Bohler's angle (tuber joint angle) measurement (normal-20°-40°. The angle in between articular surface and non-

articular surface of calcaneus) in Lateral view, is crucial in assessing calcaneus fractures. Bohler's angle, which is reduced, is an indicator of compression fracture of the calcaneus bone, which requires surgical reference.

- March Fracture:
  - March fractures, also known as stress fractures, commonly occur in the second and third metatarsals. They are often associated with overuse or repetitive stress, such as in long-distance walking, march past or running.

EXAMINATION OF PATHOLOGY ANKLE JOINT

Inspection

Attitude:

- Plantar flexion in arthritis may suggest a joint deformity or contracture.

Swelling:

- Effusion can be a sign of inflammatory arthritis, traumatic injury, or infection.

Muscular Wasting:

- Muscular wasting, especially in conditions like tuberculosis (TB), can result from muscle disuse or atrophy.

Deformity

- Charcot's joint arthropathy in diabetic patients.

Palpation

Local Temperature and Tenderness - Arthritis:

- Increased local temperature can be indicative of inflammation, as seen in arthritis.

Swelling - Fluctuation:

- This finding is particularly relevant when considering conditions such as bursitis or joint effusion.

Palpation of Bone for Local Tenderness

- Palpating specific bony landmarks, such as the lateral malleolus and medial malleolus, helps identify local tenderness and assess for potential fractures or injuries to the ankle.

Movements

- Grasp the ankle joint in one hand and the other hand proximal to the tarsometatarsal joint and check the range of motion.
- Additionally, examine the inguinal region for the presence of lymph nodes, checking for any enlargement or tenderness during palpation.

Treatment

For all fractures around the ankle, the use of a bandage with a splint or half cast below the knee is a common method to provide support and immobilization to the affected part. Bandage should be maintained up to complete reduction of tenderness, and absence of pain on weight bearing.

The decision to transition from a more rigid immobilization to a simpler bandage or orthosis would depend on various factors including the type and severity of the fracture, the stage of healing, and the individual patient's condition.

After the removal of the bandage or cast, it's indeed common to initiate active exercises and rehabilitation to restore strength, flexibility, and function to the affected joint or limb.

Period of immobilization

- Metatarsal fracture – 4-6 weeks
- Calcaneus – 3 months
- Fibula & tibia – 2 – 3 months
- Sprain – **treat the sprain as fracture**. 3 weeks of strict immobilization with posterior cast is needed in grade II sprain. Grade I sprain requires 7-10 days of simple bandage or ankle binder.

ANKLE JOINT INJURY

LATERAL COLLATERAL LIGAMENT SPRAIN

A patient with inversion injury came to OPD. Lateral collateral ligament sprain is more common than medial collateral ligament. The reason is inversion injury is more common than eversion injury. Also LCL of the ankle is weaker than MCL (Deltoid ligament) of the ankle.

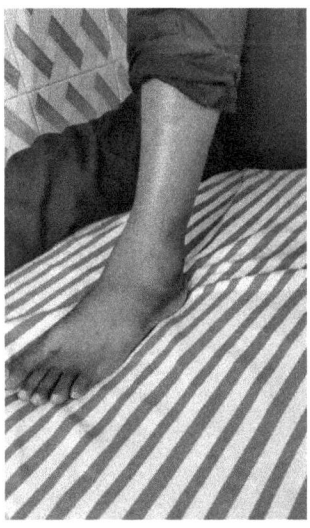

- Tomato shaped swelling
- Pain just beneath the lateral malleolus
- Pain on forceful inversion
- Springing test is negative: ie squeezing of the proximal end of the tibia and fibula (it is positive in fracture)

Lateral collateral ligament comprises three compartments; anterior, middle, and posterior compartment. Anterior is anterior talofibular ligament, middle is calcaneofibular ligament and posterior is posterior talofibular ligament. Most commonly, injury occurs at the anterior compartment of the lateral collateral ligament in inversion injury

- **grade 1:** immobilization i.e. divergent spica or ankle binder orthosis is advisable.

-**grade 2:** 3- 4 weeks immobilization along with half cast bandage below the knee for 7-14 days followed by 7-14 dyas simple bandage or orthosis as per the condition. It must be followed by rehabilitation, to avoid recurrence.

-**In grade 3** referred for surgical correction, which is rare.

NB. Surgical management of LCL of the ankle is not very common. It may be needed in sports injuries.

Bandaging in grade I LCL sprain

- The foot should be in a dorsiflexed position
- The second toe should be in same line with the tibial tuberosity
- Divergent spica type of bandaging is done
- Bandaging is done in a 90° flexed ankle joint and the heel is kept open
- After the removal of bandage, patient should start rehabilitation

To safely return to sports

- Walk and run without pain or altered pattern
- Complete 20 one-leg heel raises
- Balance on one foot easily for 30 s
- pop (jump) on one leg

FIBULA DISTAL END FRACTURE

The patient came to OPD with

- Swayathurbahulyam
- Grating sensation
- Intermittent pain

Clinical examination

- Springing positive (springing means squeezing the proximal end of the tibia and fibula, then pain over the distal end means fracture over the distal end)

Management

- Conservative management is only possible in undisplaced fracture.

This is a distal end fibula oblique fracture of the ankle.

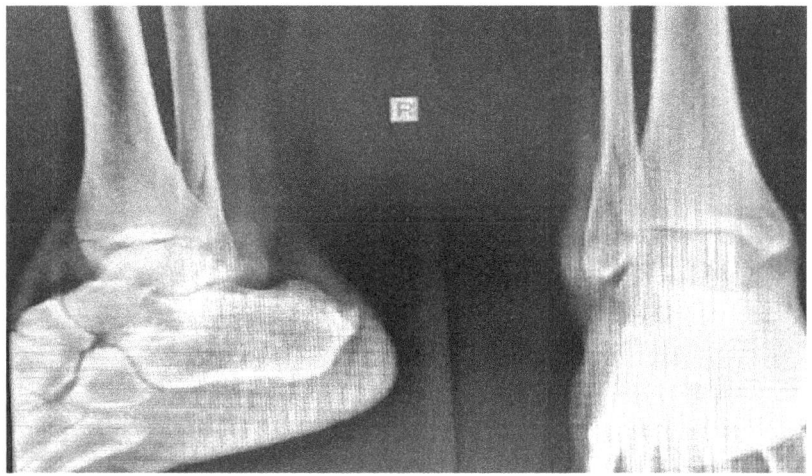

Half cast bandage

- Firstly measure from the metatarsophalangeal joint up to the knee below the tibial tuberosity posteriorly
- 15 cm POP, a total of 12 layers is taken
- An additional 4 layers of POP 10 cm is taken for giving additional stir up (medial to laterally measured below the knee)
- Then apply a stockinette. It should be fixed at the end of the bandage
- The foot should be in a dorsiflexed position and the second toe should be in same line with tibial tuberosity
- After wearing the stockinette apply murivenna, it is done to reduce pitta rakta kopa due to the fracture
- Initially, there will be hematoma formation and it is the reason for swayathur bahulyam.
- Then apply compressed cotton over the stockinette. Compressed cotton should cover the fracture site, the proximal and distal end, and the bony point; 3 layers, and 2 layers for all other sites.
- Next, immerse POP in the water. Wait for 3-5 seconds. The excessive water is squeezed out

- The 15 cm, 12 layered cast is placed posteriorly.
- Additional stir-up of 4 layers is placed medial to lateral of lower leg
- Then it's advisable to apply gauze immersed in water (squeezed out excess water) to fix the pop
- The additional stockinette over distal and proximal ends are folded and fixed with gauze
- It's better to mark the fracture site and advise the patient to pour murivenna over the fractured site.
- If splint is the choice of immobilization, total of 5 are needed : one on the lateral side, one on the anterior aspect, the medial aspect, the posterior aspect, and the other on the foot
- The half-cast bandage is more effective than a 5-splinted bandage. It gives ample support over the posterior aspect. Anteriorly murivenna shall be poured to the affected site.

POTT'S FRACTURE- BIMALLEOLAR FRACTURE OF ANKLE

There's an avulsion fracture in the medial malleolus due to the pull of the deltoid ligament or medial collateral ligament along with fibula fracture. This requires surgical correction.

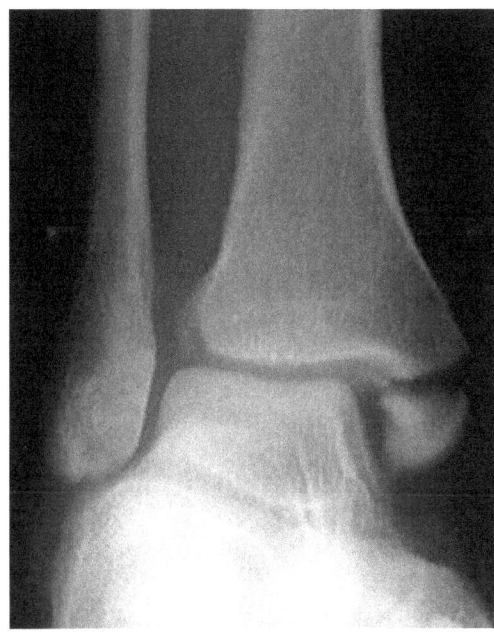 medial malleolus avulsion fracture

ANKLE JOINT PATHOLOGY
TARSAL TUNNEL SYNDROME

The patient came to OPD

- Aged 53
- The patient have numbness and paraesthesia of foot
- History of Diabetes Mellitus
- History of Hypothyroidism

It is an entrapment neuropathy just like Carpal Tunnel Syndrome. The posterior tibial nerve is entrapped in the tarsal tunnel. Due to the compression, the patient felt numbness in the 1st and 2nd toe respectively

TARSAL TUNNEL SYNDROME

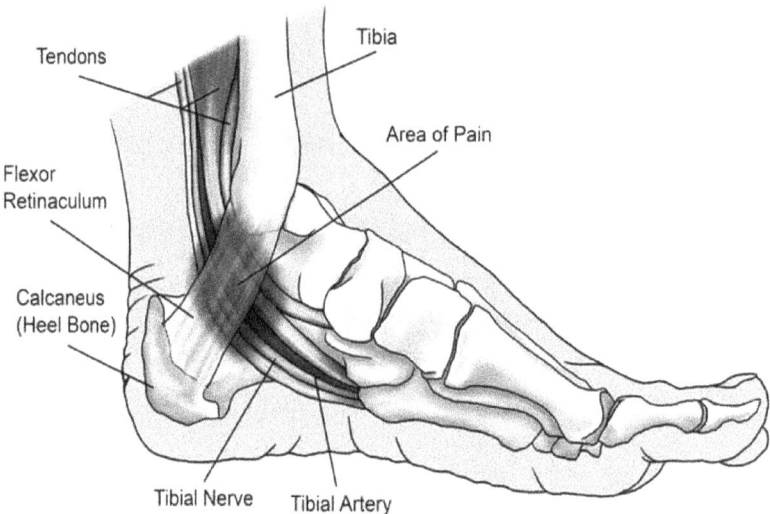

For diagnosis it's advisable to do Tinel's sign: tapping just beneath the medial malleolus and the patient feels paresthesia.

Another clinical examination is forceful dorsiflexion and eversion of the foot for 1 minute, which aggravates burning sensation, numbness, and paraesthesia over the affected area

Management

*Firstly it's recommended to address the primary diseases, Diabetes Mellitus and Hypothyroidism

*The drug dusparshakadi is effective in reducing the stenosis of entrapment

* Diuretics Punarnavadi kashaya, and Chandra Prabha are found to be effective

* After symptoms have been relieved patient should do rehabilitation like ankle pump, heel raise

* In a later stage Internal sneha prayoga should be given to avoid recurrence

OTTAWA RULE OF ANKLE[5]

Ankle and foot X-rays are prescribed in the following situations:

1. Bony tenderness along distal 6 cm of the posterior edge of the fibula or tip of the lateral malleolus.
2. Bony tenderness along distal 6 cm of the posterior edge of the tibia or tip of medial malleolus
3. Bony tenderness at the base of the 5th metatarsal
4. Bony tenderness at the navicular bone

5. Inability to bear weight both immediately after injury and for 4 steps during an initial evaluation

If it's found to be positive,

- First 2 situations requires X-ray Ankle AP and Lateral views
- Third and fourth situations demands X-ray of Foot DP and Oblique views

CASE PRESENTATION – JONES' FRACTURE

A patient came to the op with pain over the base of the fifth metatarsal followed by an injury. On giving traction to the little toe, patient felt pain over the base of the fifth metatarsal. After taking X-ray Foot, DP and Oblique, this case was diagnosed as jones' fracture and managed conservatively.

Jones' fracture is named after Sir Robert Jones, a British orthopedic surgeon who first described this type of fracture.

Key features of a Jones fracture:

Location: It is a fracture that occurs at the base of the fifth metatarsal, specifically in the metaphyseal-diaphyseal junction. This area has a relatively poor blood supply, which can impact healing.

Cause: Jones fractures are often associated with an acute injury or trauma, such as a sudden twist or impact on the foot.

Symptoms:

- Pain, swelling, and bruising on the outer side of the foot.
- Difficulty or pain with weight-bearing on the affected foot.

Diagnosis:

- Pain at base of 5th metatarsal on traction of little toe is suggestive of jones' fracture.
- X-ray Foot DP and oblique views are commonly used to confirm the diagnosis and determine the extent of the fracture.

Treatment:

- Immobilization with a below knee posterior cast for a period of 4-6 weeks
- In sports persons, this may require surgical management based on condition.

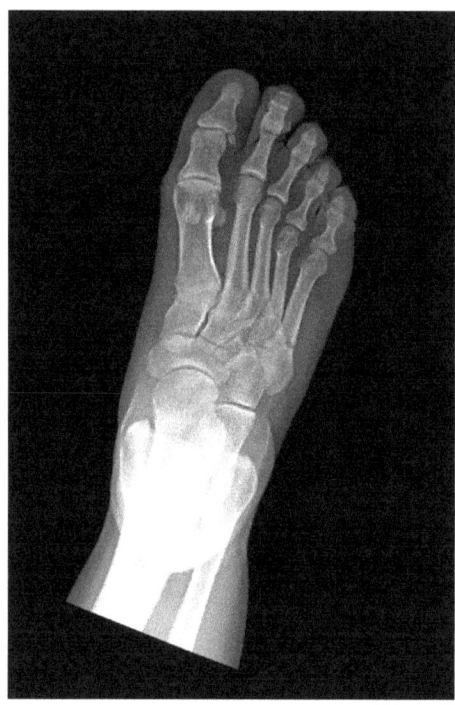

CASE PRESENTATION – PLANTAR FASCIITIS

A female patient came to op aged 45, with heel pain. She has morning stiffness and pain on walking after a prolonged rest.

Differential diagnosis

1. Systemic arthritis
2. Plantar fasciitis - most common cause
3. Retrocalcaneal bursitis
4. Achilles tendonitis
5. S1 nerve lesion
6. Haglund deformity
7. Posterior tibial tendonitis
8. Calcaneal stress fracture
9. Heel pad syndrome
10. Tarsal tunnel syndrome

Incorporating protocols designed for pathological situations and, if necessary, opting for Anusastra scientifically aligns with a comprehensive and personalized approach to patient care. Please follow this protocol in these diseases.

Diagnosis First:
- Before reaching conclusions, it's crucial to arrive at a precise diagnosis. Rule out systemic arthritis as part of the diagnostic process.

Caution with Agnikarma:
- Avoid practicing repeated agnikarma without a clear understanding of the underlying condition.

Incorporate Pathological Protocols:
- When dealing with these conditions, incorporating protocols designed for pathological situations is recommended.

Consider Anusastra Scientifically:
- If conservative measures are not yielding the desired results, considering Anusastra in a scientifically informed manner may be an option.

Footwear Correction and optimum use of orthotics:
- Correction of footwear plays a significant role in managing these conditions. Properly designed footwear can contribute to improved foot mechanics and reduced stress on affected tendons.

NB. Consider diabetic charcot foot when advising a footwear correction to a diabetic patient. Mild Heel raise in footwear should be completely avoided even if retrocalcaneal bursitis is the culprit for pain.

Physical Therapies:
- Physical therapies, including exercises to strengthen and stretch the affected area, are valuable components of the management plan.

To avoid recurrence in plantar fasciitis, there's definitely a role in pathyacharana (lifestyle modification) to avoid accumulation of ama. Application of talakkenna (head oil before bath), which is sheeta, is a potential nidana for plantar fasciitis. Hyperuricemia must be ruled out and managed accordingly.

REHABILITATION OF ANKLE JOINT
- A cylindrical ball or glass is placed beneath the plantar aspect of the foot and rolling should be done
- Ankle clench
- Single heel raise
- Heel raise of both legs
- Toe raise
- Calf stretch- gastrocnemius and soleus muscles must be strengthened

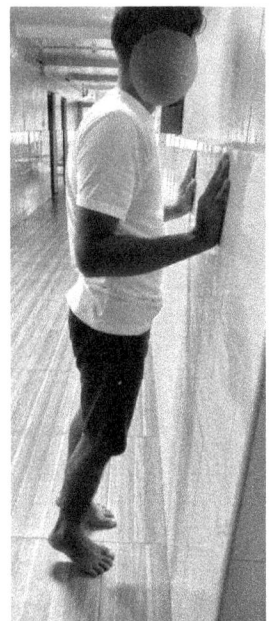 heel raise
 toe raise

 calf stretch

- First phase- **Active movements and exercises**
- Second phase- **Active movements and exercises against resistance**
- Third phase - **weight bearing, heel raise, toe raise, and calf stretch**

CONCLUSION

Our limitations, must referral situations for surgical management
- Avulsion fractures
- Femur shaft & neck fracture
- Both bone forearm fracture above the age of 14
- Fracture dislocation
- Comminuted fracture
- Open fracture
- Medial malleolus avulsion fracture
- Galeazzi fracture
- Bucket handle tear of meniscus with locking
- Unhappy triad of knee
- Recurrent shoulder dislocation with rotator cuff tear (may require reverse shoulder surgery)
- Complete tear of supraspinatus with retraction- drop arm, empty can and full can tests are positive.

Asadhya bhagna by Acharya Susrutha includes

भिन्नं कपालं कट्यां तु सन्धिमुक्तं तथा च्युतम् |

जघनं प्रति पिष्टं च वर्जयेत्तच्चिकित्सकः ||

असंश्लिष्टं कपालं तु ललाटे चूर्णितं च यत् |

भग्नं स्तनान्तरे शङ्खे पृष्ठे मूर्ध्नि च वर्जयेत् ||

आदितो यच्च दुर्जातमस्थि सन्धिरथापि वा |

सम्यग्यमितमप्यस्थि दुर्यासादुर्निबन्धनात् ||

सङ्क्षोभाद्वाऽपि यद्गच्छेद्विक्रियां तच्च वर्जयेत् (SU NI 15)

In the orthopedic clinic, evaluating and predicting outcomes through clinical examinations and relevant investigations are crucial for both injuries and pathologies. If necessary, seeking a second opinion within our field or from an orthopedic surgeon or a neuro physician is a wise move. Knowing when to refer a patient at the right time is as important as handling their conditions.

SUMMARY

Accurate history-taking is crucial when dealing with injuries and pathologies. A precise diagnosis requires a combination of thorough clinical examination and relevant investigations. Achieving a diagnosis in a single examination reflects the proficiency of a physician. Emphasizing clinical examination over excessive investigations is a commendable practice, showcasing the quality of the physician. Clinical examination coupled with prognosis holds significant importance. For instance, if the drop arm test yields a positive result, reference for surgical correction should be recommended. Similarly, in cases where a patient is unable to perform an active straight leg raise (SLR) due to a knee extensor mechanism issue involving a complete tear or avulsion fracture of the patella, prompt referral for surgical correction is ethically imperative. It is crucial to adhere to scientific principles for ethical practice, and the assessment of prognosis stands out as a pivotal factor.

The Keraleeya tradition refers to medicinal formulations typically composed of 5 to 10 ingredients, as detailed in Ashtanga Hrudaya, Chikitsamanjari, Chakradatta, and Sahasra Yoga. These formulations have proven to be highly effective in addressing soft tissue injuries and musculoskeletal conditions. To enhance outcomes and optimize efficiency, it is advisable to incorporate appropriate pathya (lifestyle modification), thereby contributing to a reduction in both time and cost associated with treatment.

In managing musculoskeletal conditions involving various joints, rehabilitation holds significant importance. The combination of internal snehapana (whether brumhana or samana), rasayana, and rehabilitation plays a crucial role in achieving sudha chikitsa (complete recovery with a focus on avoiding recurrence) for musculoskeletal pathologies.

Place constant emphasis on orthopedic neurology and soft tissue injuries. The learning process should extend from applied anatomy to orthopedic rehabilitation, encompassing clinical examination, pertinent investigations, efficient management protocols, special procedures, their indications, and the significance of internal sneha and rasayana. Cultivate the practice of offering genuine mental reassurance to patients. Incorporate the use of investigations to corroborate our clinical diagnoses. Tackle the psychological facets of pain associated with injuries and pathological conditions. By adhering to these practices, it's possible to contribute positively to the well-being of society through effective management strategies.

The concept of acquiring, sharing, and retaining knowledge can be illustrated through the interpretation of the word "**Hrudaya**":

Aaharathi: Gathering or collecting information.

Dadathi: Dispensing or sharing knowledge.

Yathi: Preserving or retaining acquired wisdom.

REFERENCE

1. Current Concepts in the Evaluation and Management of Type II Superior Labral Lesions of the Shoulder
   William A Hester, Michael J O'Brien, Wendell M R Heard 1, Felix H Savoie 1
   PMID: 30197715
   PMCID: PMC6110065
   DOI: 10.2174/1874325001812010331
2. J Ayurveda Integr Med. 2023 Jul-Aug; 14(4): 100786.
   Published online 2023 Jul 31. doi: 10.1016/j.jaim.2023.100786
   PMCID: PMC10415758
   PMID: 37531707
3. Yao K, Haque T. The Ottawa knee rules - a useful clinical decision tool. Aust Fam Physician. 2012 Apr;41(4):223-4. PMID: 22472684.
4. Classifications in Brief: Kellgren-Lawrence Classification of Osteoarthritis
   Mark D. Kohn, BA, Adam A. Sassoon, MD, and Navin D. Fernando, MD
   Clin Orthop Relat Res. 2016 Aug; 474(8): 1886–1893.
   Published online 2016 Feb 12 PMCID: PMC4925407 PMID: 26872913
5. Stiell I. Ottawa ankle rules. Can Fam Physician. 1996 Mar;42:478-80. PMID: 8616287; PMCID: PMC2146318.

BIBLIOGRAPHY

Reider B.The orthopedic physical examination.Second edition Chicago: W.B.Saunders company;2005

Joshi J, Kotwal P. Essentials of orthopedics and applied physiotherapy.Fourth edition. New Delhi: Elsevier;2020

McRae R. Clinical orthopedic examination.Sixth edition. United Kingdom: Elsevier;2010

Corrigan B, Maitland G D.Practical Orthopaedic medicine. First edition. Australia: Butterworth-Heinemann Medical;1983

White T, Mackenzie S, Gray A. McRae's orthopedic trauma and emergency fracture management. Third edition. United Kingdom. Elsevier;2016

Das S. A manual of clinical surgery. sixth edition. India: S.Das Publications;2004

Murthy S. Illustrated Susruta Samhita. 2017 edition. Varanasi:Chaukhambha orientalia;2017

Murthy S. Ashtangha Samgraha of Vagbhata. 2nd edition.Varanasi: Chaukhambha orientalia;1999

Murthy S. Vagbhata's Astanga Hrdayam. Reprinted 2012.Varanasi: Chaukhambha Krishna Das Academy;2012

Sharma R K, Dash B.Caraka Samhita.Reprint 2014.Varanasi: Chowkhamba Sanskrit series office;2014

Hamblen D, Adams J, Simpson H. Adams's outline of fractures, including joint injuries. Twelfth edition.China:Churchill Livingstone;2007

Hamblen D, Simpson H. Adams's outline of orthopedics. 14th edition.India:Elsevier Science Ltd;2009

Pubmed.ncbi.nlm.nih.gov

Orthoinfo.aaos.org

www.physio-pedia.co

Radiopaedia.org

FORMULATIONS AND PROCEDURES USEFUL FOR MUSCULOSKELETAL PATHOLOGIES

INTERNAL USAGE (TEMPLATES)

EFFECTIVE KASHAYA YOGAS IN MUSCULOSKELETAL PATHOLOGICAL DISEASES

1. PACHANAMRUTAM KASHAYA
2. AMRUTHOTHARAM
3. GANDHARVAHASTHADI
4. DASAMOOLA+RASNAPANCHAKAM
5. DHANADANAYANADI
6. ASHTAVARGAM
7. PUNARNAVADI -BOTH ACUTE AND CHRONIC
8. SAHACHARADI
9. SAPTHASARAM
10. RASNASAPTHAKAM
11. MUSTHADI MARMA- ACUTE INJURY
12. DHANWANTHARAM KASHAYA - SUBACUTE AND CHRONIC INJURY

EFFECTIVE ERANDA YOGAS IN MUSCULOSKELETAL PATHOLOGICAL DISEASES

1. ERANDA SUKUMARA
2. NIMBAMRITADI ERANDA
3. SINDHUVARA ERANDA/ NIRGUNDI ERANDA
4. GANDHARVA ERANDA
5. HINGU TRIGUNA TAILA

EFFECTIVE GULIKA YOGAS IN MUSCULOSKELETAL PATHOLOGICAL DISEASES

1. LAKSHA GUGGULU - CHAKRADATTA BHAGNA -BOTH ACUTE AND CHRONIC
2. ABHA GUGGULU - CHAKRADATTA BHAGNA-ACUTE INJURY
3. KAISORA GUGGULU - PITHA SAMANA

4. YOGARAJA GUGGULU - KAPHA SAMANA
5. TRAYODASANGA GUGGULU - TRIDOSHA SAMANA

EFFECTIVE INTERNAL SNEHA YOGAS IN MUSCULOSKELETAL PATHOLOGICAL DISEASES

1. TIKTAKA GHRITA
2. MAHATIKTAKA GHRITA
3. GUGGULUTIKTAKA GHRITA
4. RASNADASAMOOLADI GHRITA
5. BALA TAILA
6. GANDHA TAILA
7. DHANWANTHARA TAILA
8. KSHEERABALA TAILA
9. SAHACHARADI TAILA
10. KARPASASTHYADI TAILA
11. MAHARAJAPRASARANI TAILA

It's advisable to make use of matra basti if a patient is reluctant to take internal sneha orally. Definitely the absorption will be good through the rectal plexus. For the same, it's better to make use of the above mentioned taila.

EFFECTIVE RASAYANA YOGAS IN MUSCULOSKELETAL PATHOLOGICAL DISEASES

1. GANDHA TAILA
2. LAKSHA GUGGULU
3. CHUKKILIRATYADI
4. ERANDA SUKUMARA
5. TRIPHALA CHURNA
6. KAISORA GUGGULU
7. KRUSHNA TILA
8. AMALAKI
9. GUDUCHI
10. YASHTI CHURNA
11. LAKSHA CHURNA
12. SOUP WITH ASTHI, MAJJA, MAMSA

EFFECTIVE SINGLE DRUGS IN MUSCULOSKELETAL PATHOLOGICAL DISEASES

1. Vilwa moola - Aegle *marmelos*
2. Vasa moola - Adathoda *vasica*
3. Laksha - Laccifer *lacca*
4. Bala - Sida *cordifolia*
5. Sahachara - Strobilanthes *ciliates*
6. Devadaru - Cedrus *deodara*

CHUKKILIRATTYADI CHOORNAM

ചുക്കിലിരട്ടിയുറച്ചഗുളം തദ്വിഗുണന്തു വറുത്തതിലം കൂട്ടിയുരുട്ടിയൊരെട്ടുദിനം തിങ്കിലവൻ വലിയാ കുരയാ.

Ingredients
1. Nagara - 1 part
2. Jaggery - 2 part
3. Tila - 4 part

Practical use of chukkilirattyadi

- 500 g krishna tila
- 250 g jaggery
- 125 g nagara

- Mix together in the order krishna tila and jaggery first. When it binds properly, add nagara choorna. Then keep it as small balls and eat it within 2 weeks.

EXTERNAL USAGE

MURIVENNA IN ACUTE STAGE OF INJURY AND BURNS

NAGARADI LEPA IN CONTUSION

Upanaha
- For the reduction of swelling
- Advisable to use as brumhana addressing muscle wasting, with change in drugs

Dhara/ Seka
- Dhanyamla, kashaya, ksheera and taila is feasible as per condition

Shashtika pinda sweda and shashtika anna lepa
- Added with mamsa rasa

1. **Murivenna** – vamozhi yoga, kerala southern special yoga

Ingredients:

1 Kumari - Aloe *vera*

2 Palandu - Allium *cepa*

3 Paribhadra- Erythrina *indica*

4 Karanjapatra - Pongamia *pinnata*

5 Madangandhi - Borreria *articularis*

6 Thamboolapatra - Piper *beetle*

7 Shigrupatra - Moringa *oleifera*

8 Satavari - Asparagus *racemosus*

Base - Coconut oil / kera 768ml

ചൊല്ലിടാം മുറിവെണ്ണ കാച്ചുവതിനായുള്ള യോഗം നരക്ക്

എല്ലാവർക്കും തലയോടു രോഗമൊഴിഞ്ഞിടാർ പുരട്ടിടാർ തല്ലേർക്കിർ

കുഴതെറ്റി വീണിടിർ തീപ്പൊള്ളീടിർ മുറിഞ്ഞിടിർ ക്ഷതമേൽക്കിർ മറ്റു

നീരിനു ഗുദതലം വിങ്ങുന്നൊനോരർശസ്സിലും.

കറ്റാർ വാഴത്തണ്ടും അരുണിമയന്നൊരുള്ളിയും

ചെമ്മുരിക്കും മുറ്റിടും പത്രം ഉങ്ങിൻ തോലിയും ശതാവരി

താരതാവിൽ താംബൂലമേവം പറ്റും പോൽ തൈ

മുരിങ്ങച്ചെടിയിലിവതർ നീരുമായ് കാടിവെള്ളം തെറ്റാതെ

ചേർത്തെരുത്തിടും മണലാടും സമപാകത്തിൽ തെങ്ങെണ്ണ നന്നായി .

2. **Nagaradi lepa** / manikkunthirikkadi

മണിക്കുന്തിരിക്കം വചാ ചുക്ക് മീറ അരക്കോട് ചെന്ന്യായ

ചെഞ്ചെല്യം എല്ലാം കരിക്കിൻ്റെ തൊണ്ടിൻ്റെ നീരോട്

ചേർത്ത് അരച്ചങ്ങു തേക്കിൽ ശമിക്കുനു ശോഫവും.

Ingredients: Shunti, Kumari, Vacha, Laksha, Guggulu, Sala, Tankana

Effective in acute injuries, contusion, used after removal of bandage to reduce swelling if present, repetitive strain injuries

3. **Grihadhoomadi lepam**

ഗൃഹധൂമോ വചാ കുഷ്ഠം ശതഹ്വ രജനീദ്വയം.

പ്രലേപ ശൂലനുത് വാതരക്തേ വാതകഫോത്തരേ.

Ingredients: Griha dhooma (carbon), vacha, Kushta, Shathahva, Haridra, Darvi.

Indication: Vatarakta

Effective in lepa and upanaha in repetitive strain injuries prior to Agnikarma

4. **Ellumnishadi choorna lepa**

എള്ളും നിശാ മലർ കടുക്ക തുടിന്തപ്പാള നന്നാറി നല്ലമൃത് സാരണി പൂക്കിലാച

ഏരണ്ഡബീജചതകുപ്പകളും പുഴുങ്ങി പാലോടുതെയ്ക്ക സംഘ്യതം ഘനജാനുശോഫേ

Ingredients: Sesamum indicum, Curcuma longa Oryza sativa (Fried Grains), Terminalia chebula, Areca catechu (Spathe), Hemidesmus indicus, Tinospora cordifolia, Merremia tridentata, Cocos nucifera, Ricinus communis, Anethum sowa

Effective in lepa and upanaha in repetitive strain injuries prior to Agnikarma

ROAD MAP/ TIME FRAME

Injury

Grade	Cast or Splint Bandage	Simple bandage	Removal of bandage to last follow up
Grade I	No need most probably	1-3 weeks of bandage Initial internal medicines	2-3 weeks
Grade II	2-6 weeks (changes according to joint) initial internal medicines	2-4 weeks Second phase medicines	3-6 weeks

NB. A Grade III injury is typically deemed surgical. The transition from a cast to a simple bandage is always contingent on clinical examination findings. Ceasing medication, along with rasayana, is advisable once the patient regains normal range of motion and resumes regular functional activities to sustain the achieved results

Pathology

Grade	Ama pachana	Transition stage	Internal sneha	Rasayana
Grade I	1-2 weeks	1 week	1-2 weeks	1 month
Grade II	2-3 weeks	1-2 weeks	1-2 weeks	2 months
Grade III	3-4 weeks	2-3 weeks	2-3 weeks	3 months
Grade IV	4-5 weeks	3-4 weeks	3-4 weeks	3 months

NB. The progression from one stage to the next is determined by upasaya, anupasaya, and clinical examination findings. While this can be viewed as a time frame, it may not be universally applicable, especially in autoimmune diseases and neurodegenerative conditions. **Immediate initiation of rehabilitation is essential following ama pachana**.

भिषजां साधुवृत्तानां भद्रमागमशालिनाम्।

अभ्यस्तकर्मणां भद्रं भद्रं भद्राभिलाषिणाम् (A.H U 40)

www.ingramcontent.com/pod-product-compliance
Lightning Source LLC
LaVergne TN
LVHW070526070526
838199LV00073B/6709